BY THE AUTHOR OF 'EXECUTIVE PRESENCE – DEMONSTRATING LEADERSHIP IN TIMES OF CHANGE AND UNCERTAINTY'

C000109245

REMOTE
PRESENCE

A PRACTICAL GUIDE TO COMMUNICATING EFFECTIVELY IN A REMOTE ENVIRONMENT

SARAH BRUMMITT

REMOTE PRESENCE

Copyright © Sarah Brummitt 2020

All rights reserved

No part of this book may be reproduced in any form by photocopying or any electronic or mechanical means, including information storage or retrieval systems, without permission in writing from both the copyright owner and the publisher of the book.

ISBN: 978 1 78456 717 0

Paperback / Hardback

First published 2020 by UPFRONT PUBLISHING
Peterborough, England.

An environmentally friendly book printed and bound in England
by www.printondemand-worldwide.com

CONTENTS

There are a number of reasons why we all need to get serious about communicating remotely.

- So Why *Does* This Matter?
- The Global Pandemic That Is Covid19
- What We Know To Be True
- It's All About Digital Disruption
- We All Live In An 'Attention Deficit' Economy
- Organizations Are Driving Agility, Pace And Lower Costs
- We're Working And Communicating In A Different Way
- We're Working In Remote Teams And It's Not Easy
- We're Being Reduced (Quite Literally) By Technology
- We Need To Be 'Visible' In Business
- So Let Me Ask Again: Why *Does* This Matter?

An explanation of where the research comes from plus categorisation of key skills gaps.

- Where The Inspiration For This Book Came From
- Getting The Advance Communication Right
- Being Seen
- Starting A Remote Meeting Well
- Managing The Discussion
- Making Meaningful Contributions
- Ending On A High
- Keeping It Fresh
- Using PowerPoint Remotely
- Different Scenarios Require Different Strategies

I like organizing content into frameworks that make sense. This chapter helps by explaining exactly what we're talking about.   I also talk a bit about the type of 'screens' we're using when we convey remote presence.

- Defining 'Remote Presence'
- Technology And Its Impact On Our Message
- Remote Presence – The ABCDE Model
    - The 'A' Stands For Appearance
    - The 'B' Is For Background
    - The 'C' Stands For Communication
    - The 'D' Means Deportment
    - The 'E' Stands For Eye Contact
- Which 'Screens' Do We Mean?
    - Telepresence and Videoconferencing

- What We Wear Matters
- Famous Examples That Prove The Point
    - Melania Trump
    - The England National Football Team
- The Misconceptions About How We Dress At Work
- Even Zuckerberg Cares About It
- So What?
- Waist Level Wear
    - Grooming
    - Spectacles
    - Other Accessories
    - Colours On Screen
    - High Contrast
    - Pattern
    - Fit
    - Finish
    - Fabric
    - Formality

- o Different Levels Of Formality
- o Garments With No Collar
- o Garments With A Collar
- o Jackets
- o Suits
- o A Footnote On Footwear
- o Showing A Lot Of Flesh
- o The Penis Collar Jacket

There are some specific strategies around our body language that we need to get right when communicating remotely, and I explore them in more detail here.

- How We Show Up
- The Position Of Our Camera
  - o The Camera At Our Desk
  - o The Camera At A Distance
  - o The Camera In A Smaller, Breakout Room
- The Power Of The Facial Expression
- Smiling
- Looking Like You're Looking
  - o Why It Matters
  - o How To Fake Eye Contact
- Appearing Natural
- What To Do With Our Head
- Sit Up Straight
- Use Of Hands
- Our Body Language Matters Even When We're Not On Camera

Whilst you might have now been expecting a chapter on verbal communication, because there is so much to discuss, I have taken a procedural approach. So, I have linked core verbal skills and strategies to the different stages of communicating effectively in a remote environment.

- Hosting Remote Meetings
- Invitation Etiquette
- It's Good To Talk
- Who's Meeting Is It?
- Make The Invite Clear, Enticing And Dynamic
  o Purpose
  o Process
  o Payoff
  o A Word About Email Format
- Be Clear On The Meeting Objective
- Be Clear On The Meeting Etiquette
- Respect Attendees' Time
- Make Your Pre-reading Work For (And Not Against) You
- Get The Number Of Attendees Right
- Do Our Homework In Relation To Our Stakeholders
- Understand The Audience Behaviour We Might Face
- Get Our Friends Lined Up To Support Us
- Managing The Internal And External Attendee
- Decide On Our Influencing Strategy
  o Persuasion Through Logic
  o Asserting
  o Negotiating
  o Legitimizing
  o Appealing To A Relationship
- Bring Solutions, Ideas And Alignment To The Meeting
- Learn From Our Mistakes
- And Finally – Is This The Right Tool For The Job?

Chapter 7: Starting Well

In a remote environment it is essential to quickly reduce the social tension which naturally exists amongst our audience at the beginning of the remote meeting and increase rapport. Whilst this challenge is also true in a face-to-face environment, if we don't get this right remotely – and quickly – our ability to retain attention, keep our audience onside and create value is in serious peril.

- A Word Or Two About This Content
- Right Before The Meeting Starts
- The Concept Of 'Micro Moments'
- We're Judged By Our 'Hello'
- To Introduce Or Not To Introduce?
- The High Impact Introduction
- Warming Up The Room
    - o Investing In The Emotional Bank Account Of Others
- Strategies Which Work
    - o Small Talk
    - o The Scene Setter
        - Purpose
        - Process
        - Payoff
    - o Use Their Names
    - o Demonstrate Courtesy
    - o Show Appreciation
    - o Get Them Involved Early And Often (To Avoid Them Remaining Silent)
    - o Signposts Matter
- And Don't Forget...

There is so much to talk about in this chapter. Deliberately. Most of our influencing remotely relies on being outstanding here. Why? Because often we might not always be visible on screen, so the only tools in our influencing toolkit are verbal. Dip into different sections where you are interested and need takes you and enjoy yourself.

- What Underpins Everything
- The Goal Is To Be Visible
- Expand Our Linguistic Versatility

- Flex Our Tone Of Voice
- Slow Down The Pace At Which We Speak
- Avoid Rubbish Words
- Beware Of 'Management Speak'
- Beware Of Betrayal Words
- Don't Use 'Weasel Words'
- Instead, Use 'Power' Words
  - You
  - Our Name
  - Free
  - Because
  - Means
  - Instantly
- Sorry But Sorry Is Not A Power Word – Sorry About That
- Beware Of The Moving Target
- The Power Of Hyperbole
- Perfect Pronouns
- Stories: The Basis Of Any Great Persuasive Contribution
  - The Hook
    - Speak To My Priorities
    - Appeal To My Communication Style
    - Be Contentious
    - Make Me Look The Hero
    - Start With The Key Question
    - Engage With A Sound-Bite
    - Show That You Get My World
    - Show That You've Done Your Research
  - Always Have A Narrative Structure
  - Contain The Right Amount Of Detail
  - If It's Good, It's Got A STAR Moment
  - Metaphor And Analogy Can Help
  - Be Clear On The 'Ask'
  - The Iterative Ask
  - Sign Off On A High

Remote Presence

- Reading The Room
- Verbal Strategies That Add Value In A Group
  - o Making Suggestions
  - o Building
  - o Supporting
  - o Bringing In
  - o Bringing In/Shutting Out
  - o Testing Understanding
  - o Summarizing
  - o Questions To Understand Reasons
  - o Questions To Understand Feelings
  - o Being Open
  - o Defending/Attacking
  - o Giving Information
  - o Interrupting
  - o Disagreeing
- Answering Questions In General
- Answering Questions In Particular
- *The Perfect Question*
  - o The Problem With Questions
- The Reframe
  - o Keep Listening!
  - o Be Curious To Understand The Underlying Motive
  - o Change The Focus Of The Question To Find Common Ground
  - o Take The Heat Out Of It
- The Clean Answer – Avoid Too Much Information (TMI)
- Stick To The Rule Of No Nasty Surprises
- The Elegant Interruption
- Pacing and Leading
- The Constructive Challenge
- Pros And Cons

- Building A Persuasive Argument
- Wins And Learns
- The Pivot
- Making A Contribution That Counts
  - Divide It Into 3 Parts
  - Be Consistent With Energy
  - Be Relevant
  - Finish With A Flourish
- What To Say When You Don't Know What To Say
  - A Word Of Warning
  - Perspective
  - Time
  - Geography
  - People
- Things We Don't Like Saying – But Sometimes Have To
  - 'No'
  - 'I Don't Know'
  - Admitting That We Didn't Deliver The Result

Chapter 9: Other Things We Must Do To Convey Remote Presence

I've talked a lot about skills (verbal, non-verbal and visual) so far in order to be impactful remotely. In addition to these, there are best practices - which aren't skills per se - but rather 'dos and don'ts', and whilst I may have alluded to some of them (others not at all), we really must do these things consistently and effectively in a remote environment if we are to have presence.

- If We're Leading A Remote Meeting
  - Be Prepared
  - Show Initiative On The Use Of Technology
  - Stick To Time
  - Avoid Lazy Habits Regarding Remote Meeting Length
  - Achieve Your Objective
  - Offer Help
  - Follow Up In A Timely Fashion

- o Review Remote Meeting Activity Regularly
- o Invite Others To The Meeting And Kill Two Birds With One Stone

- If We're Attending A Meeting

  - o Some Easy Wins
  - o The Basic Courtesies Matter
  - o Be Visible
  - o Do Your Homework
  - o Ask Intelligent Questions
  - o Have (The Right) High Impact Introduction Ready
  - o Offer Help
  - o Avoid 'Getting On A Roll'
  - o If There Was Pre-Reading....
  - o Invest In The Emotional Bank Account Of Others
  - o Rehearse Key Messages
  - o Be A Chairman – Even If You're Not

- Why Is Storytelling On Slides So Important?
- Creating Persuasive Slide Decks

  - o Do Our Homework
  - o Have Fewer Slides
  - o Honour The Principles Of A Story
  - o Remember The 'Peak End Rule'
  - o Resist Clever Technological Wizardry
  - o Most Slides Aren't Slides
  - o Leverage The Ingredients Of An Effective Slide
  - o Using Data On Slides

- Presenting Persuasive Slide Decks

  - o Always Start With 'The 3 Ps'
  - o Sound Confident
  - o Keep Builds Down
  - o Don't Just Say What's On The Slides
  - o Verbal Signposts Are Really Useful
  - o Orchestrate The Attention Of The Audience
  - o And Don't Forget To Rehearse

Chapter One – Why This Matters

If you're a Star Trek[1] fan – and apologies to those readers who are not – then the concept of 'remote presence' isn't new to you. Amazingly enough, the idea of being able to see and talk to each other remotely via a screen was first introduced into our psyche thanks to this cult television show back in the 1960s. Watching James T Kirk, Doctor Spock and Lieutenant Uhura amongst others communicate in this way was – looking back now – extraordinarily innovative and ground-breaking. Such an approach to communication was literally decades ahead of its time, although back in the Sixties, this technique was viewed by critics of the show as being very odd, disturbing, bizarre and even an implausible thing to do. However, although business in general and the telecommunications industry in particular took a while to catch up, if we fast forward sixty years, the reality is that telepresence, teleconferencing and all other variations of communicating visually and verbally remotely via a screen are widespread business practice, a common reality of our everyday existence and are undoubtedly here to stay.

So Why *Does* This Matter?

As always, the story of 'remote presence' should begin with an explanation as to the reasons why we should care. Where to start? There is *overwhelming evidence* behind why having 'remote presence', or, being able to convey what I call 'executive' or 'leadership' or 'professional' or 'personal' presence at a distance is so *critical to having impact as a leader and influencer* in business today.

The Global Pandemic That Is Covid19

This is an additional paragraph inserted as the book was edited in early 2020. As I finished writing a three-year labour of love, the global pandemic that is covid19 has caused unprecedented chaos and uncertainty around the world. Countries are in lockdown, borders are closed, airlines aren't flying, schools, restaurants, cafes, pubs, theatres, cinemas, shopping centres are all shut, all sport has stopped, social distancing strategies have been introduced with increasing rigor and extremity, and families and friends are separated. This event will define our generation. Businesses globally are trying to balance the demands of protecting their staff and serving their clients by encouraging their staff to work remotely wherever feasible.

The social, economic and political ramifications will be enormous. Against this backdrop, all of us will spend a vastly increased amount of our professional lives working in a remote way, talking to screens where we need to drive our agenda, add value, increase our influence and get things done.

What We Know To Be True

Let's start with the most fundamental. As leaders we are in the business of change. In this era of globalization, companies are moving faster than ever. The oft-quoted expression from Google[3], (according to a gentleman from the company who I met recently), suggests that "the pace of change has never been as fast, and will never be as slow again". And where does this change start? It starts in our conversations. Conversations drive change and that's the simple truth. Whether they are formal, planned discussions lasting the duration of a planned meeting, or whether they are moments of interaction within a longer discussion, the point is that it is the quality of our ability to influence within a discussion that drives change.

Leadership is all about influence and we will fail if we can't influence remotely. It's what I call 'remote presence'. We will become invisible to others, we will waste time, we will disengage colleagues, we will have the same conversations repeatedly, we will fail to engage our team around the right story, we will experience the same problems again and again, we will move at a slower pace, we will fail to get on the radar of colleagues who don't have to do what we say, we will get told 'no' or 'not now' more often than we want, and we will get really, really frustrated in our efforts to deliver results.

Other than that, 'remote presence' doesn't matter at all. Of course, that's the trite answer. Let me be more specific because those who are as yet convinced, being able to have high impact and convey presence remotely is definitely here to stay.

It's All About Digital Disruption

We all live in a digitally disruptive age. According to Ofcom[4], the UK regulatory body for the telecommunications industry, the 'average' adult internet user is spending twice as much time – currently more than 20 hours per week – online, as compared to 10 years ago. By the time this book is in print, that statistic will already be horribly out of date. The invention of smartphone and tablet technology has led to a *dramatic* increase in internet use. Add an eye-watering expansion of entertainment media and applications into the mix with a healthy dose of vastly improved broadband speeds and there is the recipe for living online. We all used to 'go online' and now (most of us) simply live there. And of course, all of the aforementioned considerations relate to how we live our lives outside of work. It takes no account of why we might be staring at our screen for reasons to do with our professional obligations. The majority of our working day is spent glued to a screen, or in a meeting where we're easily seduced to want to look back at a screen. If we travel home on public transport, we'll notice everyone else – utterly absorbed in their technology. If we're in a restaurant, café or simply walking down the street – we see people – glued to a screen. In fact, even if we're waiting in a line, what are we doing? Checking email, posting on social media, shopping online etc. We're on our phones and on our screens all day long.

We All Live In An 'Attention Deficit' Economy

One of the most significant consequences of the rise of technology is the impact on our ability to *pay attention.* The millennial generation has known no other, as their capacity to be involved with and switch between multiple conversations, distractions and technologies is an extraordinary sight to behold. They can watch television, be on their tablet, whilst texting via an app to their friends. This level of stimuli, and responsiveness between different platforms does not come so easily for older generations, although they can learn it if they choose. Either way, the result is the phenomena of an 'attention deficit economy' as Dan Levitin's book *'The Organized Mind: Thinking Straight In The Age Of Information Overload'*[10] clearly explains. Our ability to concentrate, deeply listen and completely engage in one thing is weaker than ever before. If we transfer that reality to the world of work, here's another truth: we all know people who take the opportunity that remote meetings afford to get some work done, but none of which involves talking with other people on the call. All of us can recognize the scenario where we have been on conference calls with the button on mute as we crank through emails. We're not listening, we're not engaging with others and we don't really care very much. Why does this happen? Why are we not surprised?

My belief is that we've never properly addressed the skills of powerful communication in general before, never mind when utilizing technology to do so. Over the years, we've become used to meetings that don't deliver – just think of the reaction associated with 'having a meeting' – and then fast-forward to the 21st century. All we've done now is transfer the ineffective strategies and skills used when meeting in person to a remote meeting environment, so now it is a place that is unhelpful, and the ability to be engaging and persuasive – as well as useful – is poor. We operate in a commercial 'norm' where it is almost acceptable as a means to (not) communicate with our colleagues. No wonder we struggle to get things done. We spend far too much time in activities that are designed to encourage us to communicate, when the reality is that all too often what we are doing is achieving precisely the opposite effect.

Organizations Are Driving Agility, Pace And Lower Costs

Set against this reality is the necessity for leaders everywhere to easily communicate and collaborate with geographically dispersed individuals and teams. Historically it's been a significant challenge and historically, a significant cost.

The drive of organisations towards remote working has meant that corporate operations, R&D, sales and marketing teams, once situated in the same building, city or region, may now be scattered around the country or even around the world, thus challenging the abilities of the modern mobile workforce still further. Customers demand greater responsiveness, ease and value for money and as a result, companies respond by making business processes more efficient. Our markets have never been more competitive – and more environmentally aware – meaning that finding other ways to get business done without jumping on a plane is a powerful imperative.

Cisco conducted some research in 2009[8] - yes I know that seems like a lifetime ago in technology terms – which was aimed at understanding the potential appeal of telepresence to business, in order to advise on sales strategy amongst other things. Unsurprisingly they found that the appeal of telepresence increased with the seniority of audience. More senior leaders could easily see the appeal (and potential cost savings) of creating an environment which meant that talent did not have to traipse all over the globe just to get to meetings.

One of my clients is a global telecommunications company with whom I've had the privilege of working for 18 years. Their propositions – a wide array of mobile and fixed line communication technology – have completely transformed the way all businesses around the world connect with colleagues, teams, customers and contacts to conduct business. It has opened global markets and encouraged the evolution of vastly geographically dispersed teams, working across borders and time zones.

Mobile technology has driven efficiency, greater productivity and a lot more agility. Certainly, companies in the UK are far more open to the rise of flexible working. In fact, in some countries it is a legal requirement to offer it (should the nature of the job allow). Organizations are more disparate, and the rise of home working is doing precisely that – rising. As this book goes to print, the covid19 health pandemic means that *everyone who can* work at home, remotely, is doing so and hence this trend is being fast tracked at pace.

Greater pace, less complexity and more agility come naturally from having this media within the business. Since the advent of that research we have all been living through the effects of a global economic crisis, significant political upheaval and the breakneck speed at which digital disruption in business is doing precisely that – being disruptive. Brand new billion-dollar business have been born and built during this time, and in the same way, long established, billion-dollar brands have simply disappeared.

We're Working And Communicating In A Different Way

In the context of 'remote presence', I am struck by a number of different pieces of research that support the trend of leveraging our screens to communicate. For example, according to research at a Global Leadership Summit[18] at the London Business School in 2015, more than a third of companies reported that the majority of their workforce would be working remotely by 2020. As we read this now, how extraordinarily understated the prediction appears in light of covid19.

As countries pass the peak of the crisis, many organisations will review the necessity of having landmark properties in city centre locations, given the associated costs of so doing. Life will never be the same again.

We're Working In Remote Teams And It's Not Easy

A brilliant article from the Harvard Business Review[9] found some highly significant challenges when working with remote teams. Firstly, they found that virtual teammates are two and a half times more likely to perceive mistrust, incompetence, broken commitments, and bad decision making with distant colleagues when compared with those who work in the same location and whom they see regularly. Wow!!! I will talk a lot about trust in this book but remember the statistic. It's astounding.

If that wasn't bad enough, remote co-workers report taking five to ten times longer to address the concerns of their colleagues who work at a distance. The biggest challenge – and opportunity – is the ability to be able to create *safety* within the team so that the audience is able to open up and build a sense of trust with each other. There are so many layers to that insight, and one of them has to be that if the primary form of communication is virtual, then each remote team member needs to have a powerful and persuasive set of influencing tools to build credibility and trust with their peers when communicating remotely.

We're Being Reduced (Quite Literally) By Technology

For many years there was an often quoted, widely misunderstood study on the importance of impact, and relevance to the different facets of our communication. 55%, 38%, 7% was banded about in the wrong way. 55% of the impact of our communication was non-verbal, 38% was reflected in how we spoke and 7% was in the words we used. It was, and indeed remains, a study that all too often is incorrectly used to assert the predominance of visual, verbal and non-verbal communication, based on a famous study by Professor Albert Mehrabian[2]. The study was conducted in 1971 and let me say – like us all – the incorrect way that it's being used is getting old and we need to bring our references and rationale much more up to date.

So, I've got some new numbers for you, all of which are **fundamental** to our ability to make an impact, communicate with clarity, brevity and precision and convey presence *at a distance*. How about: 3.5, 4, 4.7, 5.1, 5.5, 7.8, 8, 11, and 12? Recognise any of these? They are in fact the dimensions *in inches* of our technology;

be it our computer, our tablet or be it our phone and there are many other variations in dimensions besides those listed. Now fast-forward to the situation where we are on screen or dialing into a teleconference. Whether it's our face taking up the full screen, or whether we are one of a host of people dialing into the virtual room, the reality is that technology vastly diminishes our size – and takes away the three-dimensional aspect. When we are communicating via a screen, we move from being our 'biggest selves' in front of others to occupying a 11' x 13' space (if we're lucky), although usually it's smaller if it's an iPad, mobile 'phone or range of conference platforms. It's like holding your thumb and forefinger apart by a distance of about three inches. That's the amount of space you now take up - plus – we go from three to two dimensions. That's a dramatic reduction in our presence – due entirely to the technology. So what? We are either now two dimensional or invisible to our audience and a wide variety of tools that we'd use to be persuasive have simply disappeared.

We Need To Be 'Visible' In Business

I have written about Malcolm Gladwell's research from *'Blink – The Power Of Thinking Without Thinking'*[7] before, and I refer to it regularly and unapologetically when working with clients. Quite simply, Gladwell quotes data in the book that supports the notion of the importance of height to impact. He surveyed approximately half the companies on the Fortune 500 list and specifically examined the height of their CEOs. Amongst CEOs of Fortune 500 companies, 58% of this audience were 6 feet or taller. This is 1.82m for our metric friends amongst us and it compared with an average across the US population of 14.5%. In addition, in general in the United States, there are 3.9% of adult men who are six foot two or taller and this compared with almost a third across Gladwell's survey sample of Fortune 500 CEOs. What I conclude from this is that, quite simply, being influential is about being visible. For those of us who are tall, then it's automatically easier to be seen. If we're easier to be seen, it's easier for us to be heard. If it's easier to be heard, then it's easier to influence.

So, Let Me Ask Again: Why *Does* This Matter?

If we link all these different pieces of information together, then I need to make a critical point when it comes to why all of us need think long and hard about the skills and strategies we need to develop to convey presence *remotely*. Historically, as an Executive Coach working on the skills of exquisite influence and persuasion, there are some consistent, robust and highly effective strategies that we coach our clients to develop:

1. We tell our clients to 'take up space' and this is very difficult because of the constraints of a laptop or smartphone screen size. The advantage of height, space and impact about which Gladwell wrote so eloquently has now been taking away from us. We're all the same 'size' on a screen, plus, that 'size' is much, much smaller than being there in person, in 'real life'. If we're only communicating verbally (so no visual), then a whole raft of skills by which to convey confidence and build trust have simply disappeared.

2. We advise our clients to adopt positive body language and this may be difficult when dialing into a conference call with either no cameras, or with 300 other colleagues on the call. Yes, I will concede that there is some data which suggests that moving around whilst speaking (when you are on a remote call with no camera), can impact the quality of your energy and delivery, however it's not *as influential as positive body language that we can all see.*

3. We encourage our clients to be crisp, dynamic and enthusiastic in tone (and yet our verbal message relies on their technology, the quality and speed of the listener's broadband connection, and ability to eliminate background noise).

4. We advise our clients to read the room to be able to flex to the needs of the audience, but we can't always see them. I call it the challenge of influencing 'the invisible audience'. It's far harder to gauge our impact on others whilst simultaneously it's far easier for our colleagues to zone out, disengage and disregard us – without our even realising it.

5. We ask our clients to be compelling, persuasive, engaging, inspiring but we also ask the audience to be *silent as well!!!!* Very often we expect a remote meeting with dozens (or even hundreds) of attendees to 'go on mute'. So, we can't see the audience and now we can't hear them. Just how difficult do we want to make this?

When we communicate remotely what technology manages to do is *drastically disrupt* the components of influence on which we have typically relied. All of these devices *actively get in the way* of our most well used components of influence, and therefore we need to understand and develop a whole new suite of strategies and skills to succeed. If we don't; then it's all too easy to just dial into a virtual meeting and crank out emails, having little interest, little contribution (if at all), and consequently zero impact. And frankly, that is what happens far too often at the moment.

The key message is this: in business, as in many other facets of our life – the behavior of us talking to screens in order to persuade others, drive change, deliver on our agenda, achieve results, be influential and get things done is on the rise and here to stay. So, we'd better be really, really, really good at it.

Chapter Two – The Research And What It Revealed

Where The Inspiration For This Book Came From

As always, my inspiration comes from my clients. Over the past three years I have conducted more than 80 in depth interviews with leaders from sectors including healthcare, oil and gas, telecommunications, retail, digital, media and law on the topic of conveying impact remotely. All of the discussions have been based around gathering qualitative data regarding their experiences, the challenges they face and what the impact of all of this has on themselves, their teams, the wider business and their customers and partners. In addition to that, I have conducted observation calls and participations calls totaling more than one hundred. As a result of gathering all this raw data, I have organized it into key areas around which successful leaders struggle themselves, or that they see others struggle with in order to convey presence remotely:

1. Getting The Advance Communication Right

This area was an unexpectedly large and emotive topic. Candidly, my operating assumption when I began the research was simply that the focus of output would be around what happens *during* the remote meeting. How wrong I was. Many interviewees expressed frustration with the following issues, and I wonder how many of these resonate with you in your business?

- Inviting people to calls by sending an Outlook invite (which it is assumed will be accepted), rather than checking options on the calendar for availability first. As a result, there was extensive frustration regarding the amount of time and effort spent trying to liaise and co-ordinate diaries. The overwhelming preference (for smaller group or 1:1 meetings) was to check with attendees in advance of issuing the invitation. A distinction was made for those larger scale calls where this activity would be simply impossible to do in a practical, agile or useful way.

- A lack of clarity regarding who owns the meeting. One organisation in particular had five leaders who spoke about a lack of integrity regarding the strategy of executive assistants sending diary invites from very senior leaders as the primary means by which to encourage maximum attendance. This contrasted with another business from the digital sector that viewed this as 'the norm'.

- Building on this insight, an interesting trait in several of the global brands with whom I work was the significance of *whom the invite came from*. So for example, a senior leader might be used as the organiser of the meeting and the person who owns said meeting. However, this was flagged as a strategy to get people to accept and attend, and in fact the senior leader had no intention (or even possibly idea) of joining the call. What does this say about the culture of the business? About the trust that exists? And what in relation to remote calls can we conclude? Well, whilst I leave you to draw your own, what is certain is that there is an opportunity to enhance the effectiveness of how to get the communication right in advance of the meeting – that is certain.

- A universal lack of clarity regarding the purpose of the meeting was reported. In other words, almost every single respondent commented on the number of occasions where they were unclear as to the objective of the session, what a 'good' result from the remote meeting might be and what the expectations of the audience were for the meeting. (This insight did not only apply to remote meetings I might add, and yet we also wonder why 'meetings' in business have a bad reputation).

- The challenge regarding the lack of goal clarity for the meeting actually had a number of subtleties to it as well. For example, what was often unclear was whether or not the remote meeting was a conversation or a download of information. This led to confusion for the audience regarding the protocol around how to join the meeting without causing disruption, how to say 'hi' to others if they're late, asking questions, being on camera, being on mute, making contributions, challenging the meeting owner and so on. Interestingly, in the absence of clarity, for those whom I interviewed the typical response was to go on mute and make little, if any contribution to it. We all also know that this means check out and do something else, like sending emails and having sidebar conversations via the chat function instead.

- Being unclear as to the purpose of the remote meeting also raised interesting questions regarding whether or not the remote format was the right media for conveying certain information. So for example, what I found during my research was that in certain situations, it would be much easier, more agile and a better use of everyone's time if the owner of the call simply picked up the phone and had a conversation with specific colleagues rather than always organize a group remote meeting. An over reliance on conference calls as *the only method* of communication is the point being made here.

- Conformity and the amount of robust, productive discussion required are worth lingering on for a couple of moments. Across a number of my observed remote meetings, it was very easy to notice (whether the audience was visible or not), the speed with which 'group think' can develop. I appreciate that the reasons for this can be many and complicated, however, time and again, I noticed a lot of people agreeing with each other. Now, it's not about suggesting that we are *trying to create situations in which we disagree,* the point is broader and links back to meeting purpose. Do we want scrutiny? Welcome challenge? Want to incorporate the perspectives of others? If the answer to these questions is 'yes', then how effective are we at ensuring that we create an environment which supports this?

- The role of pre-reading for a remote meeting represented a repeated challenge. Common examples included:
  - o Lack of preparatory time given by the meeting organiser to the invitees. This means quite simply material being sent sometimes right before the meeting. The point was that there was no time to read the pre-read! For some of us, this makes little difference (because we wouldn't read it anyway), but for others it matters – a great deal.
  - o In addition, too much pre-reading sent in advance, causing the audience to ignore it completely or simply skim it. Extended conversations and rescheduling of meetings were all mooted as consequences of this type of behaviour. A slowing down of the decision-making process was also repeatedly noticed as a result. The challenge of the (a) right format for reading material (b) the length of it (c) the story behind it were all given as examples of how pre-reading can fail to be effective.
  - o In terms of the content of the pre-reading itself, an unclear story and lack of direction around it was also commonplace. So, there was often the claim that too much information was shared, with the audience being expected to work out what they were to do with all of this

information. Several leaders were *visceral* in their frustration for being told on the call that all too often they could have skipped large swathes of the pre-read, and this is after they had invested considerable time reading and understanding it.

o The use of PowerPoint as a technology for sharing pre-read information. Many organisations have as part of their operational rhythm the use of PowerPoint to support conversations. However, there was a tendency towards too many and too dense a deck of slides that lacked a clear story and a clear 'ask'. (In addition, *repetition of this information* once on the call by going through a dense slide deck once again is a big no-no.)

- The length of time for a remote call to which we are invited is an interesting area upon which to focus. Most meetings were too long, too repetitive and not regularly or sufficiently scrutinised to ensure they were delivering value over the long term. This impacted the value of the communication in advance because habitual meetings could be 'branded' as not worth the time to attend it (and contribute to it in a meaningful way).

- Etiquette regarding the set up in advance of the call, including:

  o Confirming availability before scheduling the call, a lack of integrity regarding whose call it is (e.g. senior leader to drive attendance), number of people to invite to attend, what is the right practice around use of video and mute functionality based on the platform, over reliance on the technology (e.g. sometimes easier to call directly), when to schedule calls, when to say 'no' to calls, length of meetings, a lack of clarity regarding notes capture and distribution etc.

2. Being Seen

All too often people aren't. There are a range of considerations around this, including the platform being used, the number of people on the call, the quality of internet and intranet connection etc. Despite all of this, my research revealed:

- Endless inconsistency regarding whether or not we should turn our cameras on so that we can all be visible to each other during the remote meeting. Overall, there was a tendency *to want to avoid* turning the camera on.

- If visible, a wide array of dreadful angles, backdrops, poor lighting and bad framing of the speaker – all of which prevented a professional, effective visual aesthetic for the meeting attendees. It was all too easy for the viewer to be distracted by what they saw (and not in a good way).
- Yet more inconsistency regarding having a professional, high resolution photograph as part of our profile if we choose not to be on camera. All too often a photo was absent, but if we're not using our cameras it must be *the minimum.*

The other area around visibility related to making meaningfully contributions, and I have explained the issues which arose as a separate topic.

3. Starting A Remote Meeting Well

Etiquette and competency around the technology was repeatedly observed. In relation to etiquette there was repeated contention and frustration expressed in relation to – amongst other things:

- How much time is allowed for late attendees to join. We all have a different relationship to time, and being 'on time' varied amongst my interviewees from being five minutes early through to five minutes after the meeting has started.
- Being clear for the audience in explaining how to maximise different elements of the platform functionality during the conversation in order to drive efficient, productive discussions.
- The amount of time taken with audience introductions – and whether these should even be done – for groups beyond a certain number.
- The use of the mute function. The golden rule being to be on mute unless we want to be heard! Yes I know this is basic, but how many times recently have you been on a conference call when the leader has asked everyone to check that they are on mute.

Remember, these are all examples which fall under the category of 'starting well' and it is worth remembering that this is all before the session has even begun. It is also important to stress of course that interest and attention is high at the start of the meeting, but there's no guarantee that it will remain. Picture the scene: the meeting organiser is late to the call, they seem to be woefully unprepared, half of the audience doesn't *really know why* they have been invited to the call, there are the sounds of dogs barking, heavy nasal breathing and paper shuffling in the background. And then the host starts rambling incoherently and in an uninspired way. We nod because we just might be able to relate to it.

In truth and throughout my research, I observed a mixture of competence in this area ranging from timely, relevant and compelling set-ups to the session contrasting with boring, irrelevant comment and excruciatingly long-winded introductions from each audience member. In one conference call scheduled to last 60 minutes, attendee introductions took up the first 22 minutes. Nobody – and I mean nobody – has that kind of time.

So you see? There's a lot to consider at the beginning of a remote meeting. It just reinforces the ease with which we can make a complete mess of starting well and we would do well to remember that.

4. Managing The Discussion

By far the most common habit I observed (and continue to experience in my working life), is the ability of remote meetings to stay on time, on track and on task. This is also no less of a challenge in our face-to-face meetings I might add. Specifically my research revealed the following typical gaps in skill:

- A lack of clarity regarding agreeing and communicating the purpose of the meeting. Is this about getting a decision? Agreeing action? Garnering support? Providing information? Sharing ideas? Securing alignment? The list goes on; and the point is, *what is the point* of the remote meeting? And by the way, is this clear to everyone attending? All too often the answer was 'no'.
- Getting the remote meeting 'warmed up'. By this I mean that social tension is at its highest at the beginning of a meeting – along with our attention. If we are unable to get the group onside early by getting them actively involved, then the attention drops rapidly and before we know it, we've lost our audience.

- Being able to 'read the room' and pivot as a result. This is hard enough to do when we have the visual of our audience and we can observe facial expressions, body language and get a 'feel' for the energy and mood in the room. But what about when we're not there? It's an *invisible* audience and hence difficulties included:
    - o An inability to observe the obvious and subtle requirements of the audience. Do they know why they're on the call? Do they know what's expected of them in terms of contribution? In relation to our messaging, do they want detail or headlines? Are they interested in the customer or the competition? Do we focus our discussion at the strategic or operational level? Do they talk more quickly or more slowly? Do they use certain phraseology, certain language, cadence, rhythm in their expressions and way of speaking? Audiences that are 'in rapport' have a commonality to their verbal communication. How comfortable are they to challenge each other? Do they want the same outcomes as us from the discussion? (Assuming that's what this is). Think about it. If we are unable to see the audience and read their reactions, it's very easy to fall into consensus thinking, and get stuck.
    - o This is about knowing when and how to adapt our communication style in order to convey our message more effectively and be more influential as a result.
    - o Getting past sticking points is a real issue and there are a number of subtleties to it.
        - Getting side-tracked: this in part is the consequence of a lack of clarity of the purpose, but also a lack of confidence around how to manage the direction of the discussion and stay close to the reason for the conversation so that a productive output is reached by the end of it. Ambiguous meeting scope, a misrepresented desire to want to appear inclusive and collaborative, a concern to not want to hurt others' feelings and a singular lack of confidence and competence to demonstrate assertive, persuasive communication skills irrespective of audience seniority all played their part in this area.

- Knowing when and how to park the discussion if it veers off track, or becomes too heated or is simply not appropriate for the remote group forum is another area requiring work. The distinction in terms of skills gap from the point listed above is that there are times when the conversation needs to be brought back on track and there is no follow up, versus times when the discussion merits being paused, with a commitment to returning to it at a later stage. Unfortunately the result is still the same; that being that *too much* time is taken on a topic with a consequence being that other topics are cannot be addressed or are not given sufficient airtime.

- The opposite of this is knowing when we need to park the original agenda and spend the time on an issue which has arisen. In other words, knowing when we need to address the challenge, concern or potential 'showstopper' is essential if we're going to achieve what we had originally planned. This is made much more difficult because we can't see the audience and gauge the full extent of how they feel about things.

- Getting involvement from the entirety of the group, assuming we want it, was regularly observed. We all know that those who have something to say will be heard and will contribute. But what about the rest? All too often there is too high a proportion of the audience who have contributed absolutely nothing. Why is that? It might be because they were incorrectly invited to the remote meeting, the remote meetings goals were unclear, and/or the person hosting the meeting didn't even notice, or realise it was their responsibility to get involvement from all attendees. Or it might be that there is simply a habit, or rhythm of meeting (for example with a project team and a regular touchpoint). Everyone dials in to the remote call, but the value of it decreases over time and we're not on camera, then the email quota just goes up from audience attendees. I was amazed how often leaders told me "I don't really know why I'm invited to that meeting". We can definitely discuss the view which says that these individuals should demonstrate leadership by seeking the reason for their invite. However in any case, the person owning the meeting needs to make this crystal clear on a regular basis.

- Our ability to manage those who easily dominate through a variety of strategies (for example by leveraging seniority, getting on to their 'pet' topic, demonstrate poor ability to read the room and plough on regardless etc.) is another facet to keeping the conversation on track. There were cultural norms undoubtedly observed within this skill gap. For example, certain cultures would never dream of interrupting a senior leader or challenging a widely held view. In any event, to be effective in a business context, we need to get better at managing the behaviours of those who consciously or not like to take control.

- Handling challenge positively. As human beings we are wired to prove ourselves right once we have taken a position on an issue. It is an instinctive natural response to move into 'defend' mode, rather than remain in a state of curiosity. When combined with not being able to see or read a range of cues that might normally be available, this response becomes even more heightened and predictable.

- Speaking truth to power confidently. How to prepare for the scrutiny, hold our own, be persuasive in a way that resonates for the speaker and then move forward all require confident, cohesive skills and strategies.

- Finishing on time. At the other end of the call being able to end the meeting at the time that was agreed and not be disrespectful of others time by overrunning. Several organisations in my research cited specific individuals or departments that had built a brand reputation around poor time management for remote meetings and hence, attendance at and participation in said meetings were to be avoided like the plague.

5. Making Meaningful Contributions

There is so much within this particular area. Repeatedly my clients and interviewees talked about how all too often they observe either (a) too many people being too quiet or non-participative during remote meetings or (b) when others speak, it lacks impact or (c) too much 'talking over each other', creating an awkward, frustrating experience. There were many different scenarios and examples offered and as a result, I have outlined throughout the book a wide range of tools, strategies, tips and techniques to make sure that when we speak, we have impact.

6. Ending On A High

All too often meetings 'trail off'. This is not impactful. There isn't the same energy, impetus, sense of momentum that would encourage the discussion which has just been held, to now convert to productive action and results. In simple terms, this is about getting the job done in a timely way. If the goal of the meeting was to make a decision, then a decision is made. If the goal of the meeting is to agree action, then actions get agreed in order to drive forward implementation. If the goal of the meeting is to get commitment, then commitment is sought and given, and this is done explicitly so that all attendees know what they have just signed up to. It's all too easy for conversations to be deferred, decisions delayed and the easy option of 'let's talk about this again at another time' to be the most common recommended next step.

Instead, a sense of tension appears as the clock ticked around to the allotted finish time, or a sense of deflation, as people drop off the call because they 'had another meeting' are all contributions to a flat, rushed conclusion. This is often accompanied with a lame follow up recommendation which made the conclusion of the meeting all the more underwhelming. Is relief and a sense of delight that it's over really the primary emotion that we want people who attend our remote calls to feel?

7. Keeping It Fresh

When interviewing leaders what I observed was a sense of habit. In other words the classic 'we've always done it this way' type mentally. By definition, the technology that enables these meetings to be hosted is changing rapidly, so we at least should be open to the prospect of reflecting on and revising how we do things periodically. It means as leaders and influencers we need to stay up to date with the latest forms of technology to enable the best remote delivery of our message and the best remote environment for group conversation. One client I've worked with recently talked about their challenges working with an organisation that is using quite dated telephone conference technology. It's essential, if we want to be seen as current and up to date, that our understanding and use of technology reflects that.

One recent example of this which I am working on at present with a client is the situation where we have a message to communicate to an invisible, silent audience where we *don't really* want to have a conversation with them. Our responsibility as

19

influential communicators is to be creative. Why are we gathering 300 people onto a call in this situation? What would be much more effective would be a series of short, powerful podcasts or soundbites instead that we record and distribute. We can monitor the review of this material easily, and accurately measure those messages which are most reviewed, replayed, liked and which receive comments on company direct messaging platforms and websites.

My research caused me to reflect at length on the challenge of organisational culture. We absorb and reflect the experience of those around us. How others do this is how we do it, and so it's very easy to copy what doesn't work. In difficult times it's easy to be risk averse. We must not!!! We need to stay curious and seek advice about what would work more effectively to achieve the goals for our remote communication.

8. Using PowerPoint Remotely

The vast majority of my clients use PowerPoint to reinforce their remote message. *This is so easy to get wrong.*

- Let's start with the technology itself. Using dense visual media like PowerPoint is also subject to the vagaries of broadband speeds and internet connections. Whilst we can't control this in relation to our audience, if we are going to use PowerPoint we should be aware that this adds another element of complexity to our message. Not all internet connection speeds are the same, but hey, let's now add an embedded video into our slide deck to make it even more challenging! Or perhaps let's not.

- Secondly, organisations already know that influencing with the use of PowerPoint is a problem. Why? Because many have attempted to lay down ground-rules around their use, which include things like the provision of an executive summary slide right at the beginning of the deck, limiting the number of slides allowed for any presentation or pitch, reducing the time allotted to different leaders and topics amongst other strategies. What this indicates is that the business is already tired and jaded with this approach and that we need to be impactfully different if we're to use PowerPoint well.

- Thirdly, all too few professionals understand the value of being a great *visual communicator*. We learned how to express ourselves visually as very young children and then tend to forget all about it when we start talking. In addition, someone usually says that we're not very good at drawing/painting or any form of visual expression and hence convince ourselves that this is true.

- In spite of such approaches, I universally observed leaders who are unable to move on from the first slide, get side-tracked in detail, argue over the axis for a graph, fail to get to the end of their deck, present data without a 'so what?', overrun in terms of time allotted to them, find themselves joining a call where the amount of time given to their slot has been cut in half, and attempt to drive their message with an over reliance on extremely dense, complex and difficult to read visual material. Quite simply there is a lack of a clear, concise, visual story displayed on the PowerPoint slide deck which is accompanied with a compelling commentary.
- Knowing how to effectively balance the right amount of information on the slide versus what should appear in the notes or the appendix is another issue.
- 'Conducting' the content and the audience's attention to it is extremely important when using PowerPoint. By this I mean being able to direct the listener/viewer's attention to the right part of the data, combined with knowing when to reveal a key point is an art and a skill that requires a lot of work. If we are going to use 'builds' on slides, then knowing what's coming next, and how to sequence and segue between points requires rehearsal. Getting this wrong happens far too often and massively distracts from the impact.

As a consequence of all these skill gaps, the listener becomes wildly distracted, easily confused and readily able to disengage. We need to know how to construct a persuasive message, leverage the verbal strategies that are essential for an invisible audience *and then* we need to know how to marry the visual and verbal message for maximum *combined impact*.

9. Different Scenarios Require Different Strategies

There are a number of different scenarios in which we need to convey remote presence. Including communicating:

- 1:1 remotely using a technology platform such as SKYPE for Business, Zoom, MS Teams, BlueJeans, GoToMeeting etc.
- 1: a group remotely using technology such as that listed above.

- 1: a group remotely when everyone else is in the same room and we are online.
- 1: multiple groups in different locations.
- 1: multiple groups in different locations, plus some of the audience in the same location as ourselves.

You see? There's a lot going on. As a consequence of these categories of findings from my research, I have organised the content of this book to address each of these key areas and to do so from several different angles (forgive the pun). The topic of 'remote presence' is rich, fascinating, and multi-faceted, so please approach the content in the way that works best – starting at the beginning and working through – the old fashioned way – or dipping in and out dependent on your area of interest and specific need. I do hope you enjoy it.

Chapter Three – Some Definitions

Defining 'Remote Presence'

I debated for a really long time the title of this book and was originally going to call it 'screen presence'. When we think of the phrase 'screen presence' our mind naturally turns to the world of film. We think of actors who 'fill the screen', who mesmerise us through the physical and imagined space that they inhabit. How they look, how they sound, how they move, how they convey energy, emotion, connection. All of this 'reaches' us. It speaks to our heart as much as our head, we are touched and we are moved. They are powerful, memorable, persuasive, exciting, enriching and fulfilling to experience. And they are also theatrical.

But what if we're not trying to be the next Laurence Oliver? Of course, the explanation of 'screen presence' for actors isn't *necessarily* literal when it comes to us as professionals in business.

Perhaps the description doesn't stretch to being theatrical, and I'm not suggesting that we should be, but what I am suggesting is that we have to be engaging, compelling, persuasive and impactful. We distinctly need to 'reach' others and to do so in a way that requires even more skill because of the number of channels of communication have been removed or altered. We need to overcome the challenges which our colleagues *and* technology puts in our path so that clear, clean, relevant, timely messages are conveyed to our audience and they hear it, understand it, engage with it and are motivated to take action, make a decision or provide a commitment as a result.

It is most definitely this line of thinking that caused me to step away from the title of 'screen presence'. This book is not about trying to be an actor. Nor is it written with the intent of being a television news presenter.

Fundamentally our challenge is to be persuasive remotely; when we are not in the same room, perhaps not the same country or time zone as our colleagues. Hence, I have created a definition for what I am talking about when I use the phrase 'remote presence' or conveying presence remotely.

Specifically, this is what I am talking about. It is:

"To be persuasive and compelling in a remote environment. An ability to engage with and manage our audience through exquisite communication skills. Irrespective of the media, it is the capacity to 'reach' others, make valuable contributions and be impactful"

And 'remote presence' means that we're able to demonstrate this whether we are communicating via telepresence, conference call, podcast or good, old-fashioned telephone. Under duress, I have even included a short chapter at the end regarding email.

Technology And Its Impact On Our Message

Given that we're talking about remote presence, I came across some research that is really fascinating to understand and perhaps unsurprisingly, it seems appropriate to have been undertaken by the global media giant that is Google[26]. 'Rich media' is a term taken from the world of digital advertising, which refers to adverts that include advanced features such as video and audio. We encounter these a lot when logging on to free WIFI at airports, shopping centres, cinemas, restaurants, bars, and so on. The purpose of this media is to encourage the viewer to interact with the content. There is a dynamic component to the content that is designed to 'reach' the audience and create an emotional connection.

Face-to-face communication is perceived as the gold standard of rich media as well as the means by which other forms of communication are judged and Google's research reinforces this. In simple terms and to demonstrate the point, the study reminds us of the conventions around simply having a conversation, beginning with face to face in 'real time'. When several people engage in a conversation, we can tell by the gaze of the speaker to whom he or she is talking. If we use a pronoun such as 'you', what this does is indicate to whom the speaker is referring, and this is usually reinforced by non-verbal signals (e.g. nodding the head, gesturing with the hand and so on).

However, if we contrast this with a conversation happening where we cannot see the person (so a phone call or t-con situation). In order to offset the fact that there is a lack of non-verbal information in our message, we need to take the opportunity to enrich our message using this leaner media by focusing the qualities of our voice. We use more words to help the recipient of our message avoid misunderstanding. We use particular habits of repetition and volume of words to create layers of meaning. In simple terms, what happens is the concept *contextualization* (now there's a word). We provide more context by explicitly stating it, if contextual information is not readily available to the recipient of our message. There is certainly one big takeaway from this insight: wherever possible – we should turn our cameras on. It will help us to be clearer, crisper and more compelling. Too many clients don't like turning their cameras on and I strongly encourage them to avoid this trap.

Why am I suddenly talking about this? I do so because as leaders and influencers we're trying to get our stakeholders, team members and our horizontal leadership group to interact with our 'content' all the time. By 'content' I mean our message, our priorities, our goals, our agenda. By 'content' I mean that they interact with *us*.

'Lean media' means where the technology used has less capacity to carry information. A simple example would be to contrast talking to someone on the phone, versus sending a text message, versus sending a tweet with 140+ characters. A social media platform such as Twitter is a much more challenging place to get the tone and essence of our message delivered correctly because it is an extremely lean media to use.

Similarly, if we think about it, when we communicate, much of what is conveyed depends on the medium we use. If we are on the phone our facial expressions don't give away our feelings about the words we are saying, for better or for worse. Now if we take the verbal communication away and only have written text to work with, then this is even harder to convey or interpret correctly. For example, when we are typing an email, responding in a chat window or tweeting, there is no tone of voice that would add helpful contextual information to the sentences we write. A whole emoticon industry has built up as a result of this challenge to try and offset the potential for misunderstanding. In this form of the remote world, we also know how quickly and easily things can escalate via email and suddenly, a cast of thousands are being copied into a conversation that very few care about, but because of the visibility, there is a rampant and often unproductive need to 'save face'. As I always say, email is a very efficient media for exchanging information, but a very poor one for influencing others. And relationships don't get built there.

Remote Presence – The ABCDE Model

When assimilating content in a way that is useful, I like to work with a framework to organize core concepts around a topic, and in the absence of one, I will create it. The results of the research have enabled me to do this because it has revealed that there are five components around which to focus our efforts to convey impact and be persuasive to our audience.

The 'A' Stands For Appearance

Obviously, this means that we've got to be on camera on the remote call and visible if we're doing a podcast. What I am struck by is the extent to which professionals that I've interviewed and observed during remote calls, are reticent to put their camera on during remote meetings. If we're creating a podcast, we all like looking at people more than just slides. So, why is that? Is it because we are shy? Is it because we fear others will realise we look like we've been blown out of a cannon? Or is it because we don't know how to leverage our appearance to be more impactful? Or is it because we don't think it matters? Or is it that the cultural norms are such that typically cameras aren't switched on?

I have talked about appearance before and make no apologies for doing so again. The premise of remote communication means that we are taking away some of the elements of our capacity to influence others by not being in the room, reducing the physical presence of the audience, and so on. As a result, if we are able to harness one of the tools in our influencing toolkit *then we should do so.*

In the business world (with some specific notable exceptions by industry, culture and country), professional attire has become far more casual regarding what is acceptable to be worn to work, and the reality is that what we wear still matters. When I talk about appearance, what I mean by this is our visual signature; how we appear, how we dress to our essence, how we use clothing and accessories to communicate our brand. It's how we put consistency, strategy and intention into our choice of clothing so that we align with and do not contradict our personal brand.

What has been notable in my interviews are the number of leaders who commented that they are more likely to form a more negative opinion of someone initially if what they wear is very casual and they are working in disorganised, chaotic environment. Clearly this is bias in action, and yet it's important to acknowledge that *we all have them* and before we speak, contribute, challenge and engage our audience, the only information we have to work with is the visual component, so it's important that it conveys the message that we want the world to 'get' about us, rather than to contradict it. In a remote environment, all attendees commented that *initially trust is more difficult to build* if we can't see the other person. Alternatively, if the demands of the internet connection and technology being used mean that we are challenged to have the entire audience on camera for the meeting, *at the very minimum,* what we should definitely have is a recent, professional photograph on our technology platform profile so that we can convey a visual message about ourselves.

Our 'appearance' means the ability to effectively demonstrate *some essential* elements of getting our appearance right and being able to do so with the added dimension of working 'on screen'. Six areas around which I focus my conversations with clients are appropriate, complementary, the right colour, dressing for the screen, immaculate grooming and attention to detail. Dressing to appear in front of a screen requires us to take into consideration some of the practical considerations around clothing which is viewed through the lens of a camera and against a backdrop. Both areas have enormous capacity to work for, or against, us. I'll explore this fully in another chapter.

The 'B' Is For Background

Being visible onscreen means being seen in a context, or a frame. As a result, how we appear against our background can encourage or dramatically distract the viewer from focusing on us. My research revealed endless commentary about the books people have on their bookshelves, how tidy or not the backdrop is, and these observations reflect the natural and typical human need to scrutinize and understand the landscape which we survey.

I first began this book in 2017, and as I edit this book in spring 2020, the global pandemic which is covid19 is upon us, and the fascination with our background in a remote environment continues to grow. Much is being written across digital and printed media about politicians, journalists, television presenters and the British royal family amongst others – all of whom, like the rest of us, are social distancing and working from home. There have been a wide variety of articles filed on hysterical looking backdrops. For example, the Government advisor who has erotic art on his box room wall and in full view of the British media, the politician that sat in front of a completely empty mantelpiece – which may not seem anything special – until we realize that his first name is Hillary, and gags on social media quickly spread about Hilary's mantel (a pun on the author's name Hillary Mantel). There was the celebrity chef mocked for an extensive selection of (his own) recipe books hiding in plain sight, and the journalist who, because of his daily appearance at Downing Street press conferences, seemed to change every day the position and prominence of various articles, tomes and awards which he had won.

Anyone who thinks backgrounds do not matter are kidding themselves. So, what's the answer?

Wherever possible, a light, plain wall works best as a background and yet I am also mindful that currently, *the vast majority of us are working at home.* This may well not be possible, so in which case, keep the backdrop tidy and with minimal distraction. We must beware of too much busy-ness behind us because that draws the eye of the beholder and changes the visual aesthetic. For example, beware of sitting in front of a heavily wallpapered wall, or a gallery of photos or paintings, or overly stuffed bookshelves - all because our audience will be tempted to look at them and not us.

And of course, don't sit in front of a mirror – that's just distracting, as the reflection of the screen will just confuse the hell out of everyone looking at us, or at themselves in the reflection in the mirror.

Within the context of background, let me also take a moment to talk about lighting. We should never sit in front of a window with the light shining behind us, because we will find ourselves perfectly silhouetted. Back lighting means that our audience won't be able to see us properly and whilst admittedly, some of us are at an age where we look better in subdued lighting, we should never go for it deliberately. It looks odd and silly and suggests we don't know about or care about our visual impact. The light source should be in front of you, and so sitting in front of a window works best. Alternatively, we can use a lamp on the desk to help achieve the same effect, but please remember that only one source of light is best because if we combine both natural and artificial lighting it can wash us out.

My final comment on our background belongs – ironically enough – to the world of technology. Most video platforms have clever gadgetry which means we can change the background and do things like (a) throw a soft lens across it so that you are in sharp focus whereas everything behind you is not (b) change it to something entirely different so that you appear as if in front of a busy, light city and highway at night or in front of a national monument or in an area of outstanding local beauty. My own view is potentially controversial – whilst I appreciate the soft lens, I don't like the fake backgrounds. The exception would be if it was covering something even worse (e.g. a big window behind you and a large air conditioning unit for example). However, keep the background realistic.

Why? Because we talk in leadership about the need to be authentic in order to build trust. Conveying a visual impression suggesting that I am on the beach, at the leaning Tower of Pisa or in front of the New York skyline when I'm clearly sat in south west London in my office just doesn't make any sense and *isn't authentic*. I worry about distracting our audience and causing them to be absorbed by the background and wanting to understand that, rather than listen to and being absorbed by our message. In an ironic, utterly true and complete prescient event, as I edited this chapter a senior, global image professional messaged me – whilst she was sat in another digital meeting – and asked my professional view on backgrounds. She's not engaged with the speaker or their message because she's absorbed by a fake view of a beach. When it comes to our background, this perfectly demonstrates my point.

The 'C' Stands For Communication

How we use all of the facets of our voice for impact. I talked in my second book *'Executive Presence: Demonstrating Leadership In Times Of Change And Uncertainty'*[11] about verbal resonance. This is how we maximise the qualities of our voice to suit the occasion and the audience. It's about how we convey clarity relevance, precision and brilliance through our verbal messages. In the ABCDE model, the 'C' stands for Communication, and it means being able to do all of this *plus,* being able challenge, contribute to, connect with and 'reach' others remotely.

It's not only about *conveying our message,* it's about being able to influence others when they are conveying theirs and to harness any technology in a way that enhances, rather than detracts from our impact. In a digitally disruptive age this means taking into consideration the type of media we use, being able to flex our approach based on whether or not we can be seen and/or heard, maximising the benefits and minimising the downsides behind the platforms and packages that are common in business, as well accommodating the potential variation in broadband capacity and integrity. If we add into the mix that what is commonplace now is the 'global village' nature of our work, we need to be adept at communicating effectively with different cultures as well. Being able to work with *all of these considerations* in a consistently effective and impactful way means *that it's not easy* and I will cover a wide range of skills and strategies around our verbal communication later on in the book.

The 'D' Means Deportment

A somewhat old-fashioned word, but one chosen deliberately because it fits nicely with the acronym. Deportment is the way that a person stands or walks (if you're persuaded by the British description), and it's the way that a person behaves (if you prefer the north American version.) Either way, for the purposes of conveying remote presence, we should consider it as all of the facets of non-verbal communication (with one exception that warrants a section all on its own and is described below).

The 'E' Stands For Eye Contact

Widely misunderstood and often executed poorly, this area of our remote presence is so important to our ability to influence that it warrants a section all of its own. We can't easily influence those whom we choose not to look at. Of course, it is different when the scenario is a telephone call because no-one has visibility. However, in the screen world, there are a myriad of opportunities to 'fake' eye contact and it's definitely a fake, unless you are using extremely advanced technology. More of this in later chapters, but generally and widely eye contact is extremely poorly executed.

Which 'Screens' Do We Mean?

When I started writing this book, the need to clarify what on earth we are all talking about became increasingly apparent. Before I do so, let me issue a health warning -

as this book ages – so will the definitions because technology will continue to evolve. In a way that just reinforces the need for the skills of screen presence still further.

Initially my thought was simply the telepresence environment, so the technology for where we are seen, remotely. However, I have broadened the remit to include how we communicate through other screens as well, including when on a teleconference (so audio only) and offline (so the dreaded email and text scenario).

Telepresence And Video Conferencing

As part of my learning journey of working with leaders who like me, were getting to grips with screen technology, a simple truth has emerged. Not all technology is the same and so not all technology is created equal. There is such a thing as 'lean technologies', and these include things such as texts and email and their challenge when it comes to conveying screen presence is that they offer limited social cues.

And then there is 'rich media'. Essentially this is the use of video technology to give professionals, who are in **different** geographical locations, a real time sense of being together in a meeting **in the same place,** and these systems vary in their degree of sophistication. At one end we have the use of high-definition cameras which project onto life-size high definition screens, with high-fidelity acoustics that, in many cases, using lots of clever gadgetry that I do not understand, are able to simulate the effect of each voice coming from the video display for each participant. In other words, telepresence is a 'virtual' meeting where everyone is 'virtually' there.

The purpose here is to provide a bit of clarity. When I first started writing this book, my focus was going to be exclusively on the 'rich media' environment', however, I couldn't resist talking about email and as a result, have written a short chapter on it.

Frankly I could spend pages explaining lots of different options about the different technologies that are available. In fact, I did do that in the first draft of this book – and then I deleted because it was *deadly dull to read.*

So, when it comes to teleconferencing and telepresence, let me offer some typical examples with whom I have coached clients to enhance their remote presence. This includes telepresence rooms with multiple banks of screens, and where we are being 'shot' at many angles so that everyone can see everyone else from several different perspectives. The camera shots change dependent on noise and contribution, so there's lots of fun in relation to managing that dynamic successfully. The reality for all of us is that there are variations along the spectrum to where most of us spend our time.

I've also worked with clients where a number of people are in one location (e.g. a meeting room), and then a colleague is remote in another location (so on the screen) and with that comes a range of challenges. Equally, I have worked with clients who face the classic scenario of having a number of people in a room who they need to work with, whilst they themselves are not physically present and are also not visible (e.g. not on screen or on a telephone line). The key challenge is that it really is easy to forget they are there. Or, there is the situation where there is a camera with multiple people being visible on one screen in one meeting room, and they are in a reciprocal situation of viewing a camera of us in another room. For the purposes of this book, I will focus on what more and more of us spend our time doing, and that is using laptops that enable us to be seen and heard through our cameras and in-built microphones by our colleagues on the remote call. There are a number of different scenarios and I will speak more specifically about strategies in a later chapter in the book.

As a side note, even when we use technology platforms that enable us to see our audience (e.g. Skype For Business, MS Teams, Zoom, Slack, GoToMeeting etc.), it is fascinating to observe how often people do not turn their cameras on. Naturally there are considerations around bandwidth, the effectiveness of corporate intranets, the devices being used, the number of people on the platform for the call and so on. However, if we can be seen then this adds the potential for far more impact (if we get it right both visually and non-verbally). I have mentioned this several times already, and it is deliberate because *it is so important.*

There are different platforms which mean that we might be communicating with one person or with many visible on screen. There are many different capabilities that involve us being able to use visual presentation media (e.g. PowerPoint), video, whiteboards, chat functions, virtual break out rooms etc. This book is not about explaining how each part of this functionality works. The manufacturer provides online tutorials that are very effective in this regard. To be clear, it's not that I think that this is unimportant – far from it. If we are not able to get to grips with the platform itself, then undoubtedly our impact and presence is significantly damaged. It's simply that explaining all the elements of a platform and its functionality is outside of the scope of this book, and typically I pick that up when I work with people 1:1.

As we can see, the way in which we shape our message to be understood by our audience is very much governed by the constraints of the medium we use. If we want to compose compelling messages, if we want to make compelling contributions, if we want to hold remote meetings that are recognised as being useful and enjoyable, there is a lot to talk about in the world of the remote environment – hence the need for this book!

Chapter Four – Dressing For The Small Screen

One of the privileges of my job is the clients that I get to work with. They are bright, kind, successful and interesting people who usually, but not always, want to learn and hone their skills. As I write this particular chapter, I have had the pleasure of being on a weeklong roadshow with a law firm, travelling around the country talking about personal brand and its relevance to the world of law. I have just recently had a conversation with a young, female lawyer who wore jeans and a jumper to work, with no make-up and somewhat unkempt hair. She passionately believed that what we wear **should not** make a difference when it comes to our ability to convey impact and presence. She viewed the concept of thinking about what she wears, and what she conveys through what she wears as irrelevant, light, fluffy nonsense. Whilst she is right that it should not make a difference, our challenge is that we are talking about a societal bias, and it does.

What We Wear Matters

Like it or not, what we wear says something about us, and here's my view. What do you want us to see when we look at you? The first set of information that we use to form judgments of others is their visual appearance. No matter how liberal, respectful, inclusive we like to think we are; all human beings are wired for judgment. Get it right and we notice you; get it wrong and we notice what you're wearing. Quite simply it doesn't matter whether we believe our appearance should have no bearing on our perceived impact and credibility at work. The fact is *that it does*. We all have expectations and unconscious biases that mean that we need to get it right so that we *do notice you rather than what you are wearing.* The professional lawyer struggled with impact and credibility mainly because she looked about twelve and as if she was going shopping rather than going to work. This was not unconnected with her appearance; in fact, it was a direct result. It's simply naïve to think that we shouldn't have to think about our appearance. Of course we should. We're all pack animals; it's a survival instinct, and our first source of material on which to form gloriously incomplete, subjective, often inaccurate, completely personal and prone to bias impressions of each other is through our visual signature.

Everything that I have written above holds true if we are working alongside others in the same space. However, I think there is an added complication which makes things even more challenging when we are in a remote environment for a couple of reasons. Firstly, there is a literal distance between us and our audience that creates a sense of detachment, separation and isolation even. Secondly, the pieces of information that we use to inform our individually biased notions of trust are distorted by the fact that we are not literally in the same space. We cannot as easily read the cues, gauge the mood and flex our style. Hence, the first piece of information we have if you are on screen is the visual, and it takes on additional level of importance in our reading of the situation.

Thirdly, if you want to understand the importance of appearance, just ask anyone who is a member of the military. No matter the armed forces in which they serve, these are men and women who may well find themselves in the most extreme, physical conditions with their lives under threat at every moment. Despite this, the importance they place on their uniform and appearance is huge and their standards are exacting.

Finally, if we are working remotely at home – which is an environment where it's entirely appropriate to pad around in pajamas – then I think it's all too easy to fool ourselves into believing that it doesn't matter what we wear because for the vast majority of the time no-one at work is looking at us there. And yet, and yet, it still really matters what choice of clothes we reach for, even if our commute is the distance from the bedroom to the kitchen to the office and takes all of ten seconds to complete.

Getting up, getting dressed and making an effort is good for our mental health, creating separation in our day between different roles we fulfill and shifts our mindset more towards work. I'm not suggesting wearing a formal suit to go and work in our spare room, I am saying make an effort.

Famous Examples That Prove The Point

Melania Trump

We notice what others wear. In 2018, the US First Lady (Melania Trump), went on a surprise visit to McAllen, Texas, to visit children caught up in a dispute about immigrants being separated from their children and managed by being put in cages. This isn't the place to comment on my moral outrage around that policy. The point is that all of the media coverage was about the First Lady's jacket[23]. It was green jacket with the words *"I really don't care. Do U?"* Debating whether or not the media should have covered this choice of clothing isn't the point. What is relevant is the fact that what everyone noticed was the jacket. What was the message she was trying to convey? Is she trying to tell us something? What is the state of her marriage to the President? And – are all these questions what she and her team of highly paid media advisors would have wanted to be the focus of her trip?

As someone who appears to be deeply affected by the scandal surrounding the treatment of the children of illegal immigrants, we can reasonably assume that the First Lady went to offer moral support and also to shine a light on the situation in front of the gaze of the world's media. If it *was the case* that all she genuinely wanted was to focus on the trip, then the choice of jacket was woefully naïve. The endless tweets about #It'sJustAJacket simply didn't ring true. The irony is that the message – about not caring – is clearly her reality whichever way you look at it. She didn't care to think about the press coverage of what she was wearing (and she does have form in this area due to past missteps), and/or she didn't care of the consequences (if it was a deliberate wardrobe choice). The point is this, whatever you read about this situation, the First Lady didn't care. In addition, this sits squarely at odds with the humanitarian nature of her visit to the centre in Texas in the first place.

The England National Football Team

Another unexpected occurrence during the course of my research and writing of this book is fate of the England football team and the World Cup. Normally, writing that sentence would act as a cue to howls of derision at our woeful track record (rightly so), and the certainty that we would have exited the competition either on penalties, or at the hand of a team of part timers who had barely cobbled enough money together for the airfare. However, this was not the case. Staggeringly, when I wrote this section of the book, England were still in the competition and did in fact reach the dizzy heights of the semi-finals. So what's that got to do with 'appearance'? Quite simply the England manager, Gareth Southgate, whilst being praised for his coaching skills and the performance that he has driven out of his team, also received a wide press coverage regarding his choice of attire – namely his penchant for wearing a waistcoat[26].

My point is that we notice what others wear. Even when the nation's focus (for that read myopia, delusion, optimism, realism, tribalism, patriotism and any other 'isms' you can think of), we still found time to pay attention to, and comment at length on, what the manager of our national football team was wearing. The argument about 'haven't we got more important things to worry about?' did not, once again, hold true.

The Misconceptions About How We Dress When We Are Working

We all just have to get over it, get real and make our appearance work *for us* and not *against us*. This **is not about** making some sort of outdated stance from a more formal age of dressing that says that there are lots of rules about what you should and should not wear. It is also **not about** suggesting that style is more important than substance. In other words, as long as we look good, it doesn't matter whether or not we have the right level of capability. Again, this is all nonsense. Nor is it to suggest that this view is incompatible with the values of a business. Clothes *are not* the most important consideration for a professional. However, if we want to influence others – in person or remotely, if we want to convey impact and be taken seriously, if we really believe in what we do, then let's just get our clothing right when working at a distance, so that we can forget all about it and ensure that it does not become an issue.

Even Zuckerberg Cares About It

And if we're still not convinced, let's talk about Mark Zuckerberg, founder of Facebook. Zuckerberg has spoken at length in the past about the need to reduce the number of decisions that he makes in a day, and he explicitly linked this to his wardrobe[24]. Indeed in 2014, he posted photographs on Facebook (where else?) of his extensive collection of identical grey tee shirts and hoodies and rationalised this by saying his purpose was to make his life as clear and as simple as possible, in order to focus on making the best decisions to serve his Facebook community. Grey tees and hoodies worn with jeans and sneakers were his absolute, cast iron guaranteed uniform every, single, day. Now fast forward to 2018 when the Cambridge Analytica scandal broke, and Zuckerberg was called to testify on data privacy in front of a senate committee in the US. As an ardent fan of casual, consistent, simple dressing we might have expected him to appear in his standard uniform – grey tee, jeans and sneakers.

Not a bit of it.

Zuckerberg appeared in a light grey/blue suit, white shirt and blue tie[25]. And let's just remember, this is a man who built a multibillion-dollar business in Silicon Valley where anyone wearing a suit is positively scorned. They just don't do it. Zuckerberg knew that what he wore would matter because of his audience, the content and the message that he wanted to convey. He was taking the charges seriously and he was talking to politicians easily thirty plus years older than him, from a different generation who simply didn't really understand his business model. He knew that if he had appeared dressed as per normal, the message would be 'I don't care', 'you don't understand', 'this doesn't matter'. Zuckerberg was controlling the narrative and he wanted the audience to focus on what he was saying, rather than what he was wearing.

And of course, the challenge outlined above still applies when working with visual technology. Obviously if we are only speaking on the telephone, then no one notices (or cares) what we are wearing. For every other situation they do. And when it comes to what you choose to wear for a telepresence/conference call, then there are some important considerations as we look at you through a lens which we will cover shortly.

So What?

Clothes convey messages to the rest of the world about us whether we like it or not. This has nothing to do with fashion, celebrity or popular culture. The meaning and significance that we draw from clothing has existed for centuries and evolved over the course of them. Any professional who thinks that what they wear to work does not matter and it has no impact on their personal brand and ability to influence others is *at the very best,* extremely naïve. Humans have, and they always will, infer meaning from clothing and we all *always* have choice about what we want to convey to the rest of the world. I am uncomfortable with the language of 'dress down' and 'dress up' because of the binary nature of these terms. For a remote environment, it's all about what I term 'dress appropriate'.

We may be communicating from another office location of our business, or we may be communicating from our own home, so really, why should we care? Well, let's just address this question one last time. If we are talking to someone in another office location, there are often biases and assumptions implicit in the fact that we have made an effort to be at another work location. We've shown up somewhere else where other colleagues work so it is more easily assumed that we've tried harder. Note the bias and assumption laden in that last statement. However, if we are working at home there is bias and assumption that we've made much less effort because all we had to do was pad into our office, kitchen, dining room or wherever we choose to plug in our laptop.

Remember, the environment is remote, so a number of pieces of information have been taken away that would otherwise inform our understanding and trust of the other person and their message. Hence the tools that are at our disposal – and our visual signature is one such tool – are ones that we should choose to leverage to our advantage.

Waist Level Wear

For most of us, most of the time, what we wear matters from the waist up when it comes to remote communication, because we are sat at our desks talking to our screens. Waist level wear means some very specific principles to apply in a remote environment, and these are outlined in order of importance below. However, a couple of thoughts to share before I do so. Firstly, I have edited this section as I draft and finalise this book, so once again, I remind the reader that this part has been written as the world grapples with the covid19 pandemic. Against this backdrop, I passionately believe and want to remind the reader of the following:

1. Getting properly dressed for work each day is essential for our emotional and mental health. It's also good for the people around us at home and reassuring for those looking at us on screen.
2. We need to continue with the routines and rhythms which set our minds, spirits and bodies up for work, even when finding ourselves operating in an environment that is not normal for some of us to work for weeks at a time (i.e. at home).

3. I worry hugely about being 'too relaxed' in our attire because it creates the wrong mindset for ourselves, and we may easily and inadvertently convey the wrong impression to our colleagues.
4. Sleep attire and sportswear are so called because the clue is in the title. These garments serve functions which have nothing to do with work and we shouldn't deceive ourselves that they do; nor should we wear them when working.
5. I am married to a military man. The armed forces know better than anyone what it is like to work under the most intense, life threateningly conditions which fortunately the vast majority of us will never have to experience. In the same breath, there is no professional unit anywhere in the world in the armed forces *that does not understand, value and enforce* immaculate standards when it comes to personal appearance and uniform attire. We should all remember that and learn from it.

Grooming

I will start here because very often, and certainly during the early days of my image career, this felt like a difficult – and frankly somewhat patronising – topic to discuss with grown adults. However, because of a combination of the environment in which we are all now working, the challenge of doing so at home with other distractions, and the fact that we will (or should), be turning our cameras on, there are a number of things to consider here. Not convinced? Well, as the high definition world of a wide variety of technology platforms such as Skype[39] and Zoom[40] beckons, when the megapixels rise, so does the capacity of the audience to observe every tiny flaw in our visual appearance.

- Our hair should be tidy and groomed. Think that is patronising? I invite us all to consider how difficult this task appears to be for the current (at time of writing), UK Prime Minister, Boris Johnson. If we appear disheveled and disorganized, we are in danger of conveying that about our thinking, decision making and leadership. We're working remotely, this alone creates a new dynamic for bias and prejudice, and we want to convey the impression that we are *working* from home as opposed to *at home*. There is a difference.
- Lighting and camera angles make a huge difference to whether we appear fresh faced and well rested or whether we appear tired, rough and haggard.

Again, this is not about vanity or trying to suggest we should all look like daytime television presenters, but it is about understanding the position of camera and the natural or artificial light we are using when on screen. I have commented about this elsewhere in this book, and in addition, I *would encourage* women to wear a little bit of make-up.

- Now, before there is widespread gnashing of teeth and general fury at my last suggestion, please hear me out. *I am not* talking about applying a cosmetics counter quantity of make-up. *I am not* trying to reinforce gender stereotypes and biases in the workplace. *I am not* saying that the only way women will be taken seriously at work is if they wear make-up (plenty of empirical evidence supports this, but I digress). *I am not* betraying a woman's right to do/say/wear what the hell she likes.

- *What I am saying* is this: we can argue about how it's not right that many unconscious biases still exist at work and that times have changed etc. I agree. And – that's not the point right now. When our features are defined, it means that ironically, our audience focuses on our message, as opposed to being absorbed by how tired, young, rough we might look on screen. *What I am also saying* is that it conveys a sense of preparedness and organisation of our time and day that means others notice what we say and do, and not how we look.

- So, a slick of lipstick, a flick of blusher, some powder to reduce shine and a waft of a mascara wand does wonders for defining our features. Polished but natural is the look we're going for here. Covering dark circles works best if you apply them whilst looking down slightly into the mirror and make it an inverted triangle rather than banana shape below the eye. Light powder is fantastic, highlighters can be challenging because they get picked up more easily on the video, so beware items with high shine in them. Putting powder where we might be prone to perspire is always a good idea. As a general rule, any high shine cosmetic (lip gloss, powder, eye shadow) shows up vividly on screen and should be avoided.

- Gentlemen, powder is also good for you if you have high shine (e.g. on the top of your head). In addition, the challenge is immaculate grooming of facial hair – all of it. The 'five o-clock' shadow has a bias associated with it that we have just rolled out of bed to join the call. *I am not* saying that we can't have beards and moustaches – of course not. *What I am* saying is that camera angles and zooms can be hideous and unforgiving around nasal and ear hair; so, it should be tip top and tidy.

- A final thought on this area is to harness the power of the technology to look our perky best. Zoom[40] has an 'air brushing' feature to help everything look a little less stark. (For those who want to know, go to settings and make sure the 'Touch Up My Appearance' button is clicked. Effectively this acts to filter out blemishes and make the skin appear a little brighter. Who wouldn't want a bit of that?

Spectacles

We need to beware of lenses that glare and reflect the light to ensure that we are not dazzling our audience. Also, avoid tinted glasses because when we sit in front of natural light if this changes, so will the shades of our glasses. This means that for all of us who wear glasses, we need to make sure that we know what our glasses are doing when we are on screen. On that point, beware of choosing glasses that are too extravagant or distracting because of their boldness, colour or lack of alignment with our face shape. We shouldn't wear glasses that are the focal point of the face; we should wear glasses that in fact complement our face shape. Again, if we're not sure, hire an image professional who can help you understand our face shape, identify what we need to do to make our glasses work for, and not against us.

Other Accessories

Dangling earrings and ghastly or distracting ties (which are usually only worn if it's a very formal) are also common mistakes. A comedy tie or Christmas jumper are amusing momentarily, but utterly contradict messages of authority and credibility, so beware. Tee shirts with political slogans aren't great either. Why? Because that's what we'll keep reading and thinking about rather than your verbal message. Jangling jewellery that clatters and bangs as you move your hands and come into contact with the table can be massively distracting and annoying. Just take them off for the duration of the remote session.

Colours On Screen

The message about wearing colour is that when we wear colours that harmonise with our natural colouring, then the overall effect is healthier, fresher faced and bright eyed. When we wear colours near our face that *do not harmonise,* then we look pale, tired and/or unwell. To be clear, this isn't about vanity or fashion. It's about getting right so that our audience focuses on the message, and not on us.

In terms of colours we might choose to wear on screen, I would always recommend a note of caution when wearing white. White is a colour that glows and it can become the most noticeable thing on the screen dependent lighting, time of day, brightness of the user's computer settings, proximity to a window with natural light and background.

In addition, I do not recommend wearing bright red hues. Red is an extremely arresting (note association with the word 'arrest') and can also be very distracting. As a colour, red is definitely linked to conveying messages of power, passion, vibrancy, confidence and boldness. I love the colour; I'm just loathe to wear it on screen because it dramatically draws the eye, our audience reacts to it (largely subconsciously), and instead I advise my clients to wear it in accessories, or in a pattern, or as lipstick, rather than a large block of the colour alone.

Whenever we wear our eye colour on the top half of our body, in our choice of glasses frame, earrings, scarves, shirts, tops, knitwear, jackets, ties, dresses, as part of a pattern and so on, then it will make our eyes 'pop' and be more noticeable. This means that our garments harmonise and accentuate our natural colouring and is a good thing because again, where would we want people looking when they look at our faces?

Remember, knowing what colours suits us best is *always* useful to understand because we have to wear clothes everyday of our life. *Why wouldn't* we want to know what works and what doesn't? It's not vanity or fashion or pointless or trivial, so I would also strongly advise investing in a colour consultation with a trained image professional.

We do need to think about colour in relation to our background when we're on screen. If we wear a white shirt against a white background then we'll easily start to look like the wall behind us. My point is that it's about being mindful of the visual aesthetic and not a slave to it. The eye is drawn to contrast and seeks meaning in distinction, shape and form. So, wear colours that suit us against a pale background. If however, the backdrop colors are bolder, then we are limited to wearing bold colors because this enables the colors in our outfit an opportunity to compete with the backdrop rather than being overwhelmed by it. If we're not sure, it's very simple. Just turn the camera on before the meeting, sit in front of our screen and ask ourselves a simple question: will the viewer be looking at us, or what's going on behind us?

High Contrast

Quite simply all this means is wearing dark colour with a light colour. So, for this think: black and white, or navy and cream and so on. High contrast in western society is associated with authority; whereas low contrast is associated with approachability. If we are going to go down the very casual look (e.g. the tee shirt and cardigan), then high contrast in colour will always look better than low contrast. Trust me, it just does.

Pattern

The size, colour and contrast in a pattern is important to consider when choosing what we wear on screen. Remember, the bigger and bolder it is, the more the eye of the viewer will be drawn to that, rather than looking at our face and listening to what we say. When we get it right, people notice us, not what we're wearing. So, anything too dramatic should be avoided because the eye will be drawn to it. Equally a note of caution around small print, geometric print – which is more common with shirt fabrics and ties or jackets if it's more formal. Beware of these creating a visual distraction because of how they are represented on screen. Some patterns become fluid (i.e. they appear to move) when we look at them, which is visually distracting and confusing to the audience. Not sure? Turn your camera on in selfie mode and have a look.

Fit

Don't wear clothes that pull, gape, stretch or hang off us. Just don't do it. The visual aesthetic of it on screen is absolutely awful. It is accentuated because it fills a relatively much bigger proportion of the visual space that the viewer sees. It also screams 'I don't care', 'I'm not worth bothering with', and it reveals a lack of attention to detail. Remember, horizontal folds tell us the garment is too tight; and vertical folds tell us the garment is too big. Don't wear clothes that distract the viewer because they don't fit us properly.

Finish

In a remote environment, I'll start with the first principle – the garment is ironed. Again, I hesitated when writing this, but was reminded by four calls in the space of a week, where people are on it wearing incredibly crumbled, tired looking clothing. Please don't make these choices. Watch out to ensure that buttons, hems etc. are all be perfect and, as the name suggests, finished off properly. Stretched seams, hanging buttons, worn hems on shirt cuffs etc. means that the garment is tired and needs to be either repaired or retired. Remember, if we are on camera, depending on the technology of the viewer, their perspective of some of these apparently small things can be dramatically heightened. Our audience can see in glorious technicolor what's not working about the finish of our garments, and even the most appalling dressed observer can critique it. It says: 'I don't care'. We should.

Fabric

Quite frankly thinking about the weight, texture, look and weave of fabric are all enough to have most of us already starting to lose the will to live when considering what to wear. Plus, in a remote environment their significance is linked to the impact of wearing that fabric *through being seen on screen*. The reality is that most of us really don't spend *any time* thinking about fabric in relation to our clothes. However, when it comes to conveying the right visual signature, we should know a little bit about fabric, in order to know what will fit and flatter us best. If you don't want to acquire this information and if you are not already convinced, here's yet another reason to get the support of a qualified image professional who will give the information you need to know and nothing more.

For those of you who are interested, here is the key information: fabric can be described as light, medium and heavyweight; it can have very smooth or very rough texture and can be very loosely woven or very tightly woven. The rule is this: the more structured and tightly woven the fabric, the more structured it is and the more it should fit and follow the silhouette of our body. The more relaxed the fabric and more loosely woven it is; the more drape it has, so for example linen, cotton, linen/silk mix. The cut, weight and weave of the fabric has a big impact on how formal or informal our outfit is, and as always, we have choice.

Formality

I have deliberated left this section to the end of the chapter. Why? Because I believe that everything explained so far needs to be correctly understood and considered first, before we get down the brass tacks of then choosing what to wear for working remotely. There are some competing tensions at play here. The reality in business is that we are all dressing a lot more informally for work and gone are the days when businesses the world over were filled with people wearing suits and ties. Yes, there are some environments and industries where a suit and tie standard of dressing still exists, but this is now the exception rather than the norm. In addition, the covid19 pandemic, which is prevalent at time of writing, means that with the exception of key workers, we are all operating from home, and it makes the likelihood of wearing a tie and suit even less common.

So the simple message is this: garments have different levels of formality associated with them and as I outline a very useful framework which I have used for years below, I have deliberately included what to wear on the lower half of our body because (a) there are some remote environments which mean in the future, we may be on camera with a fully body shot, and so it will matter what we wear on the lower half of our body, and what is adorning our tootsies and (b) it's the best place in this book to write about it.

Different Levels of Formality

A very useful resource that has helped me to navigate business casual is based on the work of an international image colleague of mine – Judith Rasband from Conselle L.C and the Institute of Management. In 2000, she developed the Personal/Professional Style Scale[®5] and this framework advises a scale of dressing from tailored to untailored across four key levels. It is to her that I must credit the key messages behind each of level of attire outlined in the following four categories, so sit back, relax and enjoy the clarification.

Please remember, don't be tempted to play the 'yes, but' game. Everything you will read provides you with more choice about what our clothes convey, so enjoy understanding what these are, rather than looking to find a circumstance in which the approach doesn't apply. Our opportunity here is to actively choose how formal or casual we want to be when we work remotely.

Garments Without A Collar

These tend to be looser, less tailored a more relaxed fabric and reflects a visual aesthetic that shows curves (rather than lines and angles), in the construction of it. We are talking about clothes that may have more patterns or graphics on them and so think tee shirts, knitwear, blouses, tops and dresses all without a collar all reflect a level of dressing that Conselle L.C[5] describes as 'collarless'.

The messages being these garments are casual, easy-going, temporary, informal, agreeable, responsive and relaxed. This is a very common choice in business today, and *especially in a remote* environment. Whilst Conselle L.C[5] suggests that this is the most casually attired we can be at work, my view is that it is also becoming the most common, and dependent on the principles alluded to elsewhere in this chapter, we can still look smart perfectly presentable remotely. We can transform the look of a tee shirt if it fits, is ironed, we are well groomed, we wear with an accessory like a scarf or jewellery, put it over a jacket etc. All of these are endless, practical and entirely professional choices in front of us to make.

Interestingly, wearing 'no collar' can also mean not wearing socks! Unless you are fully visible in a remote environment, the chances are the audience won't know (or care) one way or the other anyway. However, it's worth noting that trainers, sports shoes all reside here – and again, are extremely common in business today.

Ultimately, we're on screen because we're doing something that is about being at work. Whatever the culture of our business, no-one has the aim of being thought of as an idiot because of our choice of attire. So, even when wearing the 'no collar' option, choosing a garment that isn't distracting because of blinding graphics or text, fits us properly, represents a colour that is complementary to our natural colouring and is cleaned and ironed would always be a very, very good idea.

Garments With A Collar

An increase in formality from 'no collar' is wearing a collar. For example, collars exist on untailored garments like a tee shirt, when they change to a polo shirt for example. The notion of a collar is designed to strengthen the formality by adding some structure to it. So, think about it. We can find collars on everything from formal shirts to knitwear; from dresses to tee shirts and so on. The messages behind a collar are therefore approachability, informality and flexibility. It is also an opportunity to convey the notion of influence for the first time in our choice of attire. So, a collar conveys influence, but this choice is less influential than either a suit or a jacket, and dependent on our choice of cut, fabric and colour, it will determine how formal or informal the look becomes. Wearing a collar means lots of choice and again, in a remote environment is an excellent design choice for our outfit. We can be authoritative and casual simultaneously. Shirts, knitwear, blouses, tops, blouses with a collar will all work beautifully.

Jackets

The look that is one level up from a collar in terms of formality is the jacket. The jacket remains the 'power' garment for both men and women and this is because it's usually a tailored garment that can convey both influence, but also more approachability and more informality than a suit. Endless choice on cut, colours and fabric for the jacket as it can be worn with more informal garments (e.g. casual trousers, jeans), or more formal garments (trousers from a suit but no tie or combine a jacket with a dress or skirt). Obviously the more formal, structured, tightly woven, and dark and muted in colour the jacket is, then the more formal it becomes (like the jacket of a suit). The more relaxed cut, unstructured and loose fabric with bolder pattern and brighter colours it is, then the more informal the look and message. So, lots of options, but the key garment to wear to convey these messages is a jacket. In a remote environment this does, dependent on the audience, industry and culture, tend to be less common.

Of course, if we are working at home, I'm not suggesting we wear a formal jacket as a 'go to' look, but it does mean that there are occasions when we might reach for one. As always, what we wear depends on our goals, our audience's expectations, and the culture in which we operate. If we were working remotely from another office location – and again - dependent upon the industry, the culture and our objectives for the discussion – it would be entirely appropriate and comfortable to wear a jacket. Remember, a jacket can transform our look to enhance the authority and credibility in our visual signature.

Suits

The most formally attired we can be in a professional context in western society is wearing a suit. This is the key design element and it means wearing a jacket with high contrast shirt or blouse and (usually for men, but women can too) wearing a tie. Obviously, the only way that we can convey the messages behind a suit are if we are fully visible.

We all know - in theory at least - what a suit means. These are matched garments (in other words, two or more garments made from the same fabric and in the same colour), where the fabric is more structured, tailored and smooth. Such garments are usually cool, dark colours, cut to a design with more angles than curves and combined with 'high contrast' (be that a shirt or blouse) and a tie. I wear a tie with a shirt to work for some of my more traditional clients in the City of London. The messages behind these choices of clothing are authority, formality, precision, stability and credibility.

Suits are typically viewed as the most formally attired we can be during the day at work in a western society. There are some professions for whom a suit is the workplace norm and if we were working in another office location and dialing into a meeting, then this would be entirely normal as a choice of attire. However, if we were working at home and others were in the office, then this starts to create some interesting challenges and potential tensions when it comes to choosing what we wear. Do we want to look like we fit in with everyone else? Do we want others to notice that we are working at home versus those who are dialing in from a workplace office?

I'm *not suggesting* that a suit and tie is a 'go to' working from home look. As I have repeatedly indicated, when we get it right, no-one notices what we wear. When we get it wrong, all we notice are the clothes. In a remote environment I believe this is now the least common choice of garment in business today, so whilst useful to know, I fully appreciate that it is no longer typical. How the business world has changed!

A Footnote On Footwear

As I alluded to earlier, unless we are in a full length shot then this will not be an issue. It's worth noting that what represents a more formal versus a more casual shoe reflects the same principles as those which apply for clothing. The more structured the shoe is, with stiffer fabric (e.g. leather versus swede versus cotton) and darker, neutral tones mean a more formal look. This contrasts with the opposite of this (a bright red Superga trainer for example), which is much more casual.

Not convinced it matters? In a remote environment where we are talking waist level wear then the short answer is that it does not matter one jot. However, in some remote environments it certainly will. One of my clients is a global healthcare business who offers a talent development initiative to high potential talent. Part of the process is pitching out ideas to leaders in the telepresence suite which means that they are visible in full length shot to an audience of senior leaders dialing in from around the world on their laptops.

I vividly remember one occasion where one board level executive scrutinized at length the choice of sparkling trainers worn by a mid-level manager who was part of the programme. The point is that what he wore defined him, distracted his audience, and caused precious time to be lost discussing it. Whilst one might argue that this was banter and an attempt by a senior leader to put a more junior colleague - who was in a very stressful situation - at their ease, it impacted his credibility. It also got in the way of his message and his impact. Would he rather be remembered for his shoes or his message? The answer is obvious.

Showing A Lot Of Flesh

The eye is drawn to flesh – always. There's a very sensual message behind showing more skin and that's why the more flesh we reveal, the more casual the message we convey. As I write this section of the book, a female Member of Parliament has received significant attention for being called to the House of Commons to address parliament wearing a dress that exposed her shoulder[36]. Acres of broadcast media, along with a Twitter storm and much debate amongst political commentators ensued. Whilst there is an upside – which is the dress is to be auctioned by the MP and the proceeds given to the Girl Guides - which is fantastic. However, my view is simply this: as a look it was too sexy, too revealing, too much like a 'date night' outfit. Do we want people commenting on what we wear? Not really, no. We'd much rather they were responding to what we are saying. So, to avoid that possibility stick to commonsense rules, particularly with an institution that has been around for millennia.

In addition, there are a number of potential options to consider when it comes to showing flesh. If our audience has a full body shot then for ladies, the length of our garments does matter if we're showing our legs. If our skirt or dress is too short, then our legs are where the audience will look. That is not a sexist comment; it's just a fact. If we are sat down and visible on screen, it is important that we are able to easily and discreetly cross and uncross our legs both at the knees or the ankles.

I also need to rant for a moment about cleavage. The very short answer is that we shouldn't reveal it. I have a colleague of mine who regularly shows her cleavage and whilst I can appreciate her figure from a personal point of view, from a professional perspective she looks ridiculous. It is not only unprofessional and distracting, but in a virtual environment where we are looking at her through a thirteen by eleven-inch screen for example, then the cleavage just absorbs more and more of the space. All we can see are boobs. Please, please put them away if we want to be taken seriously.

As I have written before and repeat here again without apology, get it right and we notice the person, get it wrong and we notice what they're wearing, or failing to wear in this case. So, the message is simple: don't show a lot of flesh. You have been warned!

The Penis Collar Jacket

Well I bet dear reader that this caught the eye if for no other reason than curiosity. It broke the Internet (specifically Twitter), when a television host called Natarsha Belling[35] wore a green jacket with a collar line that was shaped, like, well, a penis. I have shown the picture many times in workshops and 1:1 coaching sessions, and it's fascinating how some of my audience sees it straight away and others don't. It was an innocent mistake for sure, but boy did it mean that absolutely *no-one* who saw the visual representation *was paying any attention* to what she said.

Remember Background Is Important In Relation To What We Wear

Our background has a significant impact on what we wear and the visual image it creates as others look at us on screen. Normally this is not something that we worry about, but if we think about it, our audience is looking at us within a very specific space or frame of reference. So, what is behind us becomes very powerfully and visually part of the story. As I wrote earlier, if we are sitting behind pattern or texture (e.g. with a wallpaper if at home, and in front of a busy corporate logo if we're in a meeting room at the office), then this has much greater significance than in a face-to-face environment. The viewer can easily become distracted and visually dazzled, so if we have to sit with these types of backgrounds, we should avoid wearing pattern ourselves. We want the audience focused on what we're saying, rather than wondering whether or not they can get through the length of the call without feeling ill, laughing etc. Inevitably they will end up looking at the patterns, rather than looking at us.

In addition, don't sit with a mirror behind us because it will reflect which screens we have open and so we might get caught out if – God forbid – we are doing something else rather than paying our full attention to the call. If we have our cameras turned on and can see our audience, the viewer may be distracted to try to find their own image on the screen, rather than focus on us.

I always advise my clients to avoid sitting in front of a window because we can be silhouetted, and also to be wary of a window to the left or right side of us. Again, this is because we can create a strong light/dark contrast when looking at us, which is visually distracting to say the least.

In Summary.....

Remote Presence

I fully appreciate we are in a remote environment – and possibly not always visible because our cameras are turned off. However, as I wrap this chapter up, I'm passionate about emotional and mental health as part of being a confident and effective communicator and, like it or not, our personal grooming, clothing and accessories do play an important part in that dynamic. 'It'll do because I'm working at home', or 'it'll do for work', or 'it'll do because everyone is really casual' is simply wrong. It's work, and we want to inspire and engage others rather than invite silently observed judgment because we look tired, scruffy and unappealing. This is not vanity, narcissism or self-indulgence. This is simply about being healthy, being disciplined and demonstrating leadership. If we look like we don't care about ourselves, it is extremely difficult to convince others that we care about them. For the last time: get it right and we notice you; get it wrong and we notice the clothes.

Chapter Five – Managing The Non Verbal Message

The fact of the matter is that we're always communicating and it's largely non-verbal, and when it comes to the topic of 'remote presence', it is well worth being extremely clear. Technology experts (like communication experts come to think of it), will always argue that when we add voice *and image,* we are using much richer sources of communication. Being visible onscreen matters – as I have discussed elsewhere in this book – however it is *the way in which we do it* that is so essential to get right. I once watched a Chief Executive Officer give an entire video presentation bent over notes on a table in front of him while the audience – who were his entire organization, since this was an "all hands" event - viewed the top of his head. Then, because the camera was much too close to him, when he occasionally glanced up, his eyes were disproportionately large, and he appeared 'wild-eyed'. Trust me, the look was not a good one.

This is an example of what's important when it comes to non-verbal communication. We communicate in several languages simultaneously. We were born with the innate capability to communicate through our postures, gestures, facial expressions, and vocal capability. In fact, our brains search for and expect these most primitive and significant channels of information. According to Dr. Thomas Lewis, an expert on the psychobiology of emotions and assistant clinical professor of psychiatry at the university of California San Francisco[37], when we are not able to experience the range of cues from others, our own ability to be an effective communicator is dramatically impacted.

How We Show Up

One of my favourite questions when working with leaders is simply: "who shows up?" By this I mean what is the energy, mindset, attitude and emotion that we bring to each interaction? Literally – how are we? Such a consideration is essential in any conversation and holds true for a remote environment. In addition, how we are in any interaction is relevant even for those dear readers who like to consider themselves the most rational, logical, objective, impassive people on the planet. We *all* have emotion even if we *don't all* show it. Furthermore, whilst of course the question 'who shows up?' matters when communicating face to face, it strikes me that it takes on even greater significance when working at distance and with technology. There are so many reasons and so many implications to consider. For example:

1. Our ability to read a room is undoubtedly impacted when we are not physically in it. We now find ourselves in a 'virtual meeting room', which creates its own challenges when trying to communicate that our 'best selves' have shown up to the meeting.
2. Our responsiveness to the 'mood' of the room is altered when we are not able to read and infer from all of the micro-signals we convey that impact rapport. Subtleties around how we organize our body, what we do with our hands, breathing, and a wide host of 'tell-tale' signs regarding rapport are really hard to pick up through a screen.
3. Our agility – both to enter into the conversation, react to the contribution of others and steer the discussion is diminished (to varying degrees dependent on the technology) due to our 'size' in the room.
4. Our willingness to truly listen – and stay listening gets impacted. Many different considerations around this including the dynamic where there are several people in one room and then others dialed in. The norm around 'going on mute' to speak to each other in a breakout meeting or going off screen so as not to be seen, occurs often. I call the remote environment 'the distraction environment' for this reason.
5. The speed of the technology itself. There is not enough space to talk about the differences in broadband and fibre optic capability dependent on where we are in the world, save to say that the variation is startling.

This topic matters because as leaders, we have the responsibility to create the environment. I saw a brilliant clip of the incomparable comedienne Ruby Wax[16] who conveyed a mantra that sums up our responsibility as leaders and influencers in business. Quite simply as leaders it is our responsibility to create the environment when communicating with our colleagues. We can make it toxic, or we can make it so good that the audience will do anything for us. As we explore the topic of body language, we would all do well to remember that.

The Position Of Our Camera

There are a number of scenarios here – some of which we can control and some of which we cannot. These include the typical 'talking to our computer on our desk' situation, which is something we can absolutely change to our advantage. However, I am also mindful of other scenarios which range from wall mounted monitors in small breakout rooms, to cameras placed high up in a corner of a larger meeting room, which means we have to work with what we've got.

The Camera At Our Desk

I will always be a big fan of turning the camera on. So, with that thought in mind, how close we sit to the camera has a massive impact on the range and degree of exaggeration we need to adopt when using our bodies to reinforce our verbal communication. The first thing I explain to a client is how the camera's distance affects the way we look to a viewer. If we position ourselves too close to the camera (as the CEO did in the earlier example), every expression and gesture will be exaggerated because of the wide-angle lens in, or mounted on, our computer.

If the camera is above the screen, then dependent on the height of our chair and angle of the screen, we'll always appear to be looking up. This is certainly much better than having a camera at an angle so that we're looking down into it. Remember, this is never, ever a good look, and if unsure, then turn your phone camera on, turn it around to selfie mode, and then look down. You'll see what I mean.

Ideally, we want to raise or lower our monitor and/or seat so that the camera is naturally at our eye level (or very slightly higher). Always remember that a lack of eye contact reduces our trust and satisfaction as the audience with the interaction, so we have to learn the skills to fake it successfully. More on that in a moment.

We also need to consider the distance of the camera from us when we're in the situation of sat at a desk talking to the screen on it. Our challenge is to make sure that we do not sit too close, because this makes us look disproportionately large and slightly menacing. Equally, not too far away either. So, my recommendation is to sit arm's length (8 – 10 inches) from our laptop or phone, with the best results where the screen-image frame starts a little above our head and ends at or slightly above waist level.

If we are using a phone, then please use a stand, because it's discombobulating for the audience to have us continuing moving around when we are on camera. It's impossible for us to keep the camera completely still if we simply have it in our hand.

The Camera At A Distance

If we are working in a meeting room with the camera mounted high on a wall, at a distance from where we are sat, then we need to put more exaggeration around our gestures, but use fewer of them, than if we are sat at our desks, right in front of the camera and the screen.

In this latter scenario, we have more options with different non-verbal communication strategies, but we can't be too exaggerated with our body language because our audience are 'up close'. There is a frame through which we are viewed by our audience, and if our movements are too expansive, it is both distracting and confusing because it looks visually odd when our hands might disappear off the screen, or our arms get truncated when we move. However, we can use head movement and facial expression because we are right in front of the camera. The opposite is true when we are a distance away.

Still not sure what I mean? Turn on your camera on your laptop, sit right in front of the screen and start moving your head, arms etc. Now take your chair and put it 15-20 feet away. You're smaller, but more of you is in shot. Your gestures need to be bigger in order to have impact. When you are up close you must not be so exaggerated.

We should sit as close to the camera as possible in this situation because sitting at the back of the room will make us visually appear very small. Remember, if it's wall mounted up high then our goal is to make ourselves appear bigger, so more visible. This means sitting as close to the camera as we can.

The Camera In A Smaller, Breakout Room

Where we sit matters because the relationship of our profile. Are we 'side on' or fully facing the audience? Are we closer to or further away from the camera? All of this will be apparent to us if we look at the display of course, and my recommendations include:

- Even if the table is at an angle to the camera, we should move our chair to be facing our audience 'front on'.

- We should be strategic about where we sit. The middle of the room/table is where the audience will naturally be drawn to look.
- Hands visible, not hidden.
- Laptops/devices away! If we have to refer to a device do so *very* briefly and then return to looking at the camera. If we want to persuade and influence others, then there is *almost no chance of doing so* if we communicate very clearly that they are not worth our full attention. If we do need to answer a quick message – acknowledge it and then actively put it to one side to show that it's no longer a distraction to us. If we are using our laptop to make digital notes, then say so and continue to regularly contribute; otherwise our audience just thinks we're doing emails.

The Power Of The Facial Impression

There has been a lot of old, tired, misquoted nonsense written about non-verbal communication and its impact on our perception of others which has caused me to pursue research that is more current in this area. For this I needed to look no further than research by Cornell University in 2016. Specifically, the work of Professor Zayas[44], a professor of psychology at Cornell University, explored the impact of first impressions and firstly what she and her colleagues found was that there is a long-lasting impact of first impressions, based on the other person's appearance. In addition, the research revealed that people continue to be influenced by another person's appearance even after interacting with them face-to-face. First impressions formed simply from looking at a photograph predicted how people felt and thought about the person after a live interaction that took place one month to six months later. Like it or not, the research shows that we still do judge a book by its cover.

Smiling

In addition, we should think about our smile because "facial appearance colors how we feel about someone, and even how we think about who they are," said Zayas[44]. Her research also included experiments that invited participants to look at pictures of women with neutral versus smiling expressions. They were then asked to evaluate whether or not the participants would be friends with the women in the pictures and to forms views on likeability, emotional stability and willingness to embrace new experiences. It reinforces our need to make sense and make judgements about the world around us in the absence of all the information.

Now, why should we care? Because in remote environment, we might spend quite a large proportion of our time looking at the faces of others and *relatively little time* hearing them speak. So, our facial expression matters.

If we smile too often or too extensively then this looks odd, reduces the trust of the audience and lacks credibility. If we don't smile at all, then this can increase tension and anxiety. My view is that the topics up for discussion have an impact on the amount we smile. For example, the debate was around laying off staff, then I can't think of a single reason why we'd want to be smiling. Showing some emotional intelligence to read the remote room is essential.

Looking Like You're Looking

This is probably one of the single biggest differences we can make to our non-verbal communication and it is *amazing to me* how often this is just badly, badly done.

Why It Matters

The importance of eye contact is found in the myriad of verbal expressions that we use in everyday language. Seeing 'eye to eye' with someone to reflect the fact that we get along; someone being 'the apple of our eye' would suggest that we hold them in high affection; 'turning a blind eye' to deliberately ignore or disregard something; 'keeping our eyes peeled' to suggest actively seeking to find something. The list is endless.

My point is simply this: these expressions are widely used and understood because of the fact that how we use eye contact is a critical component of the level of trust that exists between us and those at whom we look. I talk with my clients about the belief that eye contact is the most intimate, non-touching gesture we can make to other people.

Not convinced? Well think about getting in an elevator (or lift for our European friends). Proximity without intimacy is a very stressful human condition. Where do we look in that lift? Anywhere but at strangers who are right there in front of us.

I live in London and travel on the tube regularly. The carriages are organised so that people sit opposite each other and to avoid discomfort, tube map information and a myriad of adverts are organized above the heads of those sat opposite us. Why? So that our discomfort at being tempted to look at, and catch the eye of, those sat opposite us is avoided.

Anthropologists call eye contact a 'synchronizing signal', which means that it acts as a means by which to engage, influence and get feedback on the quality of communication from others. We also don't just stare at other people and when we 'catch the eye' of a stranger; our immediate reaction is usually to look away.

So, eye contact matters *and here's the conundrum. We can't literally look at each other on a remote call. By that I mean we can't look into their eyes and they be simultaneously be looking into ours. It's not possible.* However, what we can do – if we do it well – is fake it. My research and experience of what happens at the moment is very simply this: we don't look at each other. We look at people looking to our left, our right, up above our head, or down to the left or right. What are our audience looking at? Not us that's for sure. Typically, most people are actually *looking at themselves.* Or alternatively, they're looking at where our image is displayed on their screen if we have turned our camera on. It's very odd and disconcerting because we don't feel like they *are looking at us.* Think about it.

How To 'Fake' Eye Contact

There are some specific strategies that will mean we are looking like we are looking at other people, but our challenge here is significant. I am very mindful that there are some nuances based on the technology platform, however the conundrum for most of us, most of the time, is that in order to look like we're looking at people (in the eye) on the screen, what we actually have to do is *not to look at them.* By that I mean that we mustn't look at the display of other people, and we need to resist the allure of looking at ourselves. Instead, we need to look at the green light of the inbuilt camera at the top of your display screen. Or, if we have an additional camera separate to that, then we need to look at where it's mounted. That's the only way to show the other person that you're looking at them. The irony – and hence difficulty – of this challenge is that it means that you're *not* looking at the display of the person's face at all. Tricky isn't it? The best strategy to help is to put your display of yourself right under the camera and sit a little further back in your chair, so that incorporating both easily is the best option. We also need to practise it because looking at a tiny dot isn't natural or easy to do.

In addition, and as always, balance is required because we don't want to appear to be 'staring' at others all the time. We would not do that if we were face-to-face, so during the remote conversation we can create natural breaks in our eye contact to allow us to observe others by looking at them on our screen, referring to our notes etc. to make it appear and feel natural. As a slight aside, I use post-it notes for key messages which I need to convey and stick them around the screen for easy reference to help ensure I keep eye contact high and get my key points across during the discussion.

Appearing Natural

Since we're talking about appearing natural, research has discovered that participants in videoconferences tend to be more influenced by heuristic cues – such as how likeable they perceive the speaker to be – than they are by the quality of the arguments presented by the speaker. This is attributed to the higher cognitive demands that videoconferencing places on viewers.

When you are the presenter, you will want to guard against looking stilted and emotionless or (as I've seen too often) "over-acting," since distracting mannerisms and facial expressions will all be picked up on camera. Instead, stay relaxed and mentally picture the viewer. Doing so will help you naturally express nonverbal signals of empathy, likeability and warmth – such as leaning forward slightly, smiling, and showing the palms of your hands when you gesture.

What To Do With Our Head

The position of our head matters because everything about our physical position and movement conveys meaning. So, starting at the top, with our bonce, the goal here is for the head to be straight, rather than tilted when we speak to convey authority. Now, this seemingly small suggestion seems quite straightforward and easy to do, but in fact it is not. This is because none of us are truly symmetrical. We are all asymmetrical and the majority of us don't even realise it. My husband is just like his Dad in that his head 'leans' to one side from the top of his neck. Yes I know this sounds odd but it's true. He didn't believe me until after I had mentioned it to him, and he confirmed my opinion by checking out his profile whilst running on a machine at the gym.

Back to the head tilt. Why is this relevant? Well, if you peruse advertising online and in print media, the majority of headshots – be they male or female – show a tilted head and that is deliberate. When we adopt this posture, we expose the neck, which is a submissive gesture. It comes from being pack animals and the gesture is used to represent 'no threat'. It is amazing to me how professionals for whom being on screen is their career fail to sort this out. A well-known journalist for the BBC continually appears on camera with her head lilting and tilting to the side and I find myself yelling at the screen. When we need to convey authority, credibility and impact then keep the head straight. When we want to show that we are listening, or wish to communicate empathy, understanding and connection, then we can tilt away.

A side-note on this topic, women lean their heads to the side more often than men and it's particularly important to be careful about this when we are communicating with a male dominated audience. It can be perceived as 'weak' and ineffectual. Tough to read I know, but true, nevertheless.

Sit Up Straight

Being 'smaller' doesn't work when it comes to conveying impact and remember, we've already been massively reduced in size in a remote environment. So, we need to sit up straight and sit tall. This simply means raising ourselves up to our full seated height and not slouching. In addition, it's important not to fidget, but actually it's incredibly easy to do this continually. Self-grooming (such as scratching, hair fiddling etc.) never looks good on screen and so is to be avoided. That said, just think about when you are not on screen and just sat working at your desk. Actually, we self-groom often.

In terms of the 'shape' of our posture, we are aiming to form an open diamond, with our arms down, and with our thumbs and forefingers lightly joined in order to stop our shoulders from moving around a lot when we speak. It's important to bring animation to the face (especially the eyes), to support the notion of conviction, belief and energy. Otherwise we quickly 'drain' the energy and interest of others and our plausibility and impact lessens. The only occasion where as a strategy this will work is when you **don't want** people to remember what you said. When would we ever want that as a strategy? No, I've no idea either. If you slump, look tired and convey low energy then we are instantly forgettable. How have we shown up? Badly. It's better to not even join the call in the first place.

Use Of Hands

Joe Navarro in his brilliant book *'What Every Body Is Saying'* explores the importance how we use our hands. In truth, our hands reveal our inner state and the degree of emotional turmoil we experience at that exact moment. Remember, it is our hands that shake when we're nervous and it is our hands that sweat when we're under pressure. Quite simply our hands tell the world how we really feel at any point in time.

We also need to consider the visibility of our hands in a remote environment. Navarro talks about the importance of our audience being able to see our hands because it conveys confidence, certainty and congruence with how we feel. When we hide our hands what we are communicating is the opposite of that.

Some great examples to reinforce the point come from the world of politics. Early in his career, President Bill Clinton used excessive hand gestures which was perceived as odd and implausible to his audience. He was coached to hold his hands within a space called 'the box', which is like drawing the said shape from the width of the shoulders, down the body to the waist and to keep his hand gestures within that space. As a result, the messages conveyed were perceived as far more truthful and trustworthy.

The use of the 'ball' for our hands is where we shape them so that they are slightly cupped, and we move them around the shape of a ball (unsurprisingly). This is associated with conveying dominance and being commanding. Why? Because we are communicating a confident sense of having all the information we require at our fingertips. As always, it is in our language, whether it is verbal or non-verbal, that we reveal how we feel.

If our palms are facing upwards, then anthropologists will say that we are open and accepting, whereas palms down communicates strength and being assertive.

President Obama often used this gesture often after moments when his audience had responded rapturously to what he said, and he needed to encourage them to settle down.

In a remote environment, we should think about the screen as creating a frame within which to move our hands. The first thing to say is that we must ensure our hands aren't *too close* to the camera. If they are, our hands will look disproportionately large and peculiar because of the wide-angle lens in it. Hands need to be a reasonable distance away from the camera in order to maintain visual perspective.

In addition, when it comes to hand gestures we need to think about the view from the perspective of the audience. If we take our hands so wide that they are off camera, then this will look odd because our hands disappear; and it will look as if our arms have been truncated. What works is to keep the range of hand movements to the width of our body. This is as a good guide as any for the degree to which we can move our hands about on the horizontal spectrum. Equally, when we think about the vertical axis, raising our hands up so that they can be seen when using them to reinforce a point, is essential. Otherwise what the audience sees is some movement from the shoulders, potentially the upper arms, but nothing else and once again, this will look extremely peculiar.

When not using them to gesture, we should place our hands on the table or desk, or, if we're communicating with a camera at a distance, where people can see them. Keep them relaxed and separated. Don't hang onto the edge of the table, or we will look desperate. Don't fiddle with our pen or shuffle papers because we'll look like a newsreader. We can keep a preview window open to check how we look to the remote viewers, but don't get absorbed by continually looking at ourselves there.

Resting our hands on our chin, whilst having them intertwined in a relaxed fashion can look very persuasive in terms of conveying 'I'm listening'. We have to combine this with looking at the lens!

Our Body Language Matters Even When We're Not On Camera

I have recently coached a client from a specific part of Europe that is associated with being very calm and pragmatic in their cultural style. Entirely laudable qualities which we would not want to change. Their challenge related to impact in a remote setting.

Remote Presence

This senior female leader had repeatedly received the feedback which suggested she was bored and boring in her delivery of a message. To the audience she came across as flat, lacking in energy and utterly unenthusiastic. The consequence was that people tuned out, readily disengaged and found her utterly uninspiring.

Now, whilst it's easy to say: "be more enthusiastic!", it's much harder to just do it. Here's where our body language comes in and where the need to build different muscle memory and strength with our body has a huge impact on our verbal delivery. So, we focused on getting her to change her body posture and increase movement when conveying her message in a remote environment. Please note, this is in the situation where the camera is turned off obviously, because it would look very odd to say the least if she was walking backwards and forwards in front of her screen. However, be in no doubt that it makes a *huge* difference. In addition, through a series of exercises we worked on smiling more and increasing her mouth and jaw muscles to put more strength to project greater vocal emphasis. The difference was spectacular and authentic. Our body language matters far more than we might think. We need to make it work for – and not against - us in a remote environment.

Chapter Six – Preparing In Advance For Success

Hosting Remote Meetings

I have written elsewhere in this book about the amount of confusion and frustration that resides *in advance of the remote meeting itself,* and my research prompted me to create a specific chapter as a result. It would appear that our ability to be an effective remote communicator is already in danger of being seriously impeded before we've actually opened our mouths. My angle for this chapter is the situation where we are the host of the meeting and as such, it is focused on best practices that work to increase our impact and influence as the leader responsible for making this work well. I will cover areas large and small, tactical and strategic, all of which make a difference to the ability for our remote meetings to be effective, enjoyable and achieve what we need them to achieve.

Invitation Etiquette

As leaders our role is to be influential across horizontal teams, colleagues, senior leaders, partner organisations, suppliers and customers. Typically, what we do when joining a new company, team or project group is to observe the norm and then start to replicate it. For example, activities such as checking diaries before issuing invitations, selecting times of the working day for such meetings, duration of such meetings and a host of other areas about which I comment below and make specific recommendations. My point is this, *I would strongly suggest that invitation etiquette is an opportunity to connect and demonstrate leadership – especially given that we're talking about remote communication.*

It's Good To Talk

If we want to understand how our teams *feel,* then just ask about remote meetings and stand back. It's as if we're lighting a match. *Everyone* has a view. Whether we are talking about our horizontal teams, our reporting line, our project groups, our suppliers or partners, the chances are that it's been a while - if at all - since we've discussed what others do and do not want when it comes to scheduling meetings. I have a global client that operates project teams throughout its organisation, and whilst they are very familiar with the concept of talking about communication as part of the set up to the project, have systematically failed to translate that activity to something that is discussed *both throughout* the lifetime of the project, and also when thinking about collaborating with other groups on a regular basis. As a result, some leaders and some remote meetings across this global client have a brand association of being dull, pointless or too lengthy. The only reason people join is because it's a great opportunity to get other work done.

Another consideration is that we should gauge preferences for critical groups, individuals, colleagues and leaders that we need to influence *first* before starting to flood their inbox with invitations to meetings. Our curiosity must cover things such as start times for a meeting and frankly, this is only polite given that we work globally, duration, use of PowerPoint and other technology, frequency, objectives and value derived from hosting these remote sessions.

And we shouldn't just do this once.

It's essential as a leader to regularly seek feedback on our remote sessions and distinguish feedback on the content from the way in which these sessions are conducted. All too often over the course of my research I have gathered insights which reflect things like "don't know why I'm on the call; I don't see the point of this; no-one asks me if this is convenient or useful first before inviting me and they just expect me to show up etc."

There is a distinction of course when we might be hosting an 'all hands call' to a larger community or a larger part of our existing team. I am not suggesting we canvas every single person's opinion – far from it. In fact, I view this as an opportunity to understand how connected we are with our audience and how well we know what works, and what does not, for them.

Always remember that an effective leadership rhythm is to regularly audit the quality of the meetings we schedule – whether they are face to face or remote.

Whose Meeting Is This?

Many leaders have assistants who organise their calendars, and many projects have regular catch up sessions running over a period of time. However, what all too easily can occur are instances which reveal that:

- There is a lack of trust regarding who owns the meeting. One global client of mine spoke extensively of a tactic whereby a senior leader's name was used to encourage/mandate/coerce people in to attending said session, however all too often that senior leader was not present and not involved on the subsequent call.
- A habit of running meetings with groups of people for whom the value of the meeting is not clear – especially over time, and the person who owns said meeting is not clear – or willing – to step up and own both the meeting and the lazy or ill-conceived agenda which accompanies it.
- A lack of goal clarity for these meetings. All too often there is a conversation remotely which concludes with a decision to have another conversation – again, remotely.
- A lack of rhythm regarding auditing and changing the sequence, length and content of remote meetings to fit the changing needs of the business and the people who are supposed to attend these meetings.

Here's my view: if we have to resort to covert tactics (e.g. leveraging someone else's name or position to get people to join the call), then we have *an ocean of work* to do – starting right now. Let's think about it for a second, what we are saying is that no-one wants to come to our meetings. *This means that they don't see any value from them.* The only people who use coercion successfully are dictators, and with a bit of luck they get toppled in time. This approach to remote meetings is a damning inditement on our culture and we need to start changing it. Own the meeting, be explicit on the goal, make it relevant and appealing to our audience, deliver value during the remote session and follow up on commitments and actions to demonstrate progress. By doing this consistently, we can start to build a brand which is about creating value as we collaborate with our colleagues, rather than it having become something which others view as a great opportunity to crank out a load of emails.

Make The Email Invite Clear, Enticing And Dynamic

Time for a personal rant. If we send outlook invites without anything contained in them, then my personal view is that we should expect others to rightly disengage, ignore, attend only under duress and resent you for it. Think about it for a second. We are asking for the most precious and finite resource that any of us have to give –

and that's our time. Agendas are only very slightly interesting to me. All too often they are a lazy alternative to some precise and concise thinking. It's like sending the route map without revealing the destination. Why do we need this call now? What is the point of this? What are we going to achieve? What do you need from me? Why am I here? All perfectly valid questions as far as our invitees are concerned. No meeting, either remote or face to face, should have the purpose as 'going through an agenda'. We need to be explicit on our email invite about the goal, the format for the remote meeting and the benefits to the audience in attending and contributing to it. So, our email invite should be clear, enticing and dynamic. That means it needs to clearly communicate three things:

- **Purpose:** What is the objective of this meeting? Think in terms of decisions that need to be reached, action that needs to be agreed, commitments that need to be sought and approved. Be clear and very specific about what the goal for the remote session is and stick to it.

- **Process:** How do we want the audience to engage with us? Is this a 'cascade' type call where I sit and listen? Or do you want me to participate? Can I ask questions? Get involved? Challenge? Can we get a copy of the slides? Who's capturing notes? How much interaction via chat do you need from me? The audience needs to know, and we need to tell them. If they need to prepare, what is it they need to prepare? Can we interrupt if someone is pitching? How do we interrupt? If they need to contribute, then where, how, about what would you value the most input? Be clear, be clear, be clear on the process because these are the kinds of questions that our remote audience will have.

I talk elsewhere about the importance of 'process', however given that you are here dear reader, I will reiterate something which I believe is very important. In a remote environment with large audiences we may well be facing what I call the 'invisible audience', because we just can't see all of them. In addition, if it's a cascade message where we don't actually want them to engage in a conversation, then they are also the 'silent audience'. *So, let's just hang on a minute.* Do we really want large numbers of people dialing into a call where they can't be seen or heard? The short answer is: no. So, I invite brevity, clarity and creativity here – including recording a short message to post on an intranet portal or as a podcast. In the latter we can prepare the conversation to cover what we know will be the key questions that the audience are bound to have. However, it's much more interesting and appealing if it's a podcast. Alternatively, it may be that the message needs to be communicated to key individuals who then need to own and cascade the message themselves. Whatever the message, outcome and scenario, we need to think about the right process for communicating our message and be clear.

- **Payoff:** What's in it for me by attending this remote meeting? Why should I care about this? Why should I make time in my day for this? Why should this be something that I want to willingly engage with? Rather than resent you for adding to the number of things I need to do during my day. We need to be clear and not assume our audience already knows this. Trust me, they don't.

A Word About Email Invite Format

- o Use bullets
- o Articulate the purpose, process and payoff (the 3 Ps!)
- o Avoid lots of long lines of text – they won't be read properly, if at all
- o Keep it concise

Be Clear On The Meeting Objective

I am mindful that I have explained the notion of the objective in the 3 'Ps' above. However, it's *so important* that I want to return to it for a moment. My research repeatedly revealed that this was not clear. Are we making decisions? Agreeing actions? Giving commitments? Remember, remember, remember the habit of sending agendas, being vague, having 'catch ups', doing 'check ins on progress' etc. is rampant in business today. We haven't got time to 'have an update on what's going on in ABC account'. Please, don't fall prey to this really bad habit. We rarely have time to 'just catch up'. Our meeting objectives must be specific, measurable, relevant and achievable by the end of the meeting. Vague thinking leads to vague conversations.

Be Clear On The Meeting Etiquette

Isn't it amazing how opaque this is? Do we put our camera on or do we not? What happens if we join late? What about 'saying hi' to people when we join, because it would be rude not to wouldn't it? And do we say 'hello' because we always say 'hello' if we were meeting face-to-face, right? There are a myriad of things that can cause a meeting to be derailed *even before it's really got going.* This is where we need to show leadership and we can start that process by being clear on these things **in the meeting invite.**

It doesn't have to be lengthy and certainly it's not intended to be pompous. Far from it, the goal is to help everyone by being clear on some of the meeting etiquette. For example:

- Advise a software update check in advance.
- When joining the meeting – please turn on the camera and microphone ahead of the start of the session so we can catch up in real time.
- Advise the amount of time in advance of the start time as when we'll open the meeting to enable that catch up time and resolve technical issues. Even if it's only ten minutes, it's an offer and some will take it; others will not.
- If we're late to a meeting, please turn on the camera and *start* on mute.
- Use the chat function to say 'hi' to people if we're late arriving.
- Put any advance reading in the chat function so that people can download it and review if they've joined late, joined early, want to check something whilst others are talking etc.
- Put a welcome note in the chat function on arrival – to reiterate some of these key points concisely.
- Advise on how we'd welcome contribution. Is it by using the 'hand up' function? Or simply jump right in and come off mute? The point is: we need to take the lead here.

Respect Attendees' Time

Another common theme repeatedly highlighted in my research was *the length of the remote meeting.* Very commonly leaders reported was that the same content could have been covered in half the time or less. Does every meeting need to be scheduled for an hour? Even longer can be a terrifying prospect. The fact that we aren't in the same room, and often may not be able to see the other person, plays havoc with our attention span. Lengthy, remote meetings that are scheduled also tend to encourage a relaxed approach to arrival on time. Sounds obvious I know; but it's amazing how much time is wasted by waiting for others who can't be bothered to join for the start of the session. Always remember that our brand as leaders is impacted by how we run our remote meetings.

Scheduling fifteen, thirty, forty five minutes meetings and sticking to just that time is commonplace. The shorter the better in the world of digital commerce. Facebook are renowned for ten minute meetings. The other point about this is that we tend to schedule on the hour or half hour, and providing an opportunity for attendees to have a short break between yours and what may well be other meetings is a genuinely powerful benefit. Meetings also don't always have to start at the top or bottom of the hour either. Interestingly, meetings are rarely scheduled for quarter past or quarter to the hour. However, if we are managing our calendars well, and doing others a favour, this is an excellent way to create a short break between meetings and a chance for people to finish and get prepared for their next remote session.

Make Pre-reading Work For (And Not Against) You

Another area of challenge where the most common issues reported were (a) it was sent ten minutes before the session (b) it was sent in time but not read (c) it was sent it in time, it was read, but it didn't make sense (d) it was sent in time, it was read, it made sense *but,* it wasn't referenced, used or relevant to the subsequent conversation during the remote meeting.

My observations are don't send pre-reading unless it really makes sense to do so, *and if we do,* we absolutely have to use it meaningfully during the remote meeting. Clarity regarding whether this is a meeting about making a decision, taking action or seeking commitment should drive decisions about what content is sent in advance. In addition, it should be sent with time to read, and it should be laid out as a clear, concise story. Remember, why are we sending information at all? If it's not *to influence others* – then what is the point? Beware, beware, beware of information overload and the 'here's a load of data and words, work out what it all means for yourself' style of communication. Sending information for the sake of having the information is a classic opportunity to share via an email. Then we can decide whether or not we'll read it, ignore it and delete it.

During the meeting itself we use it. Pre-reading is an aide to making the remote conversation *go faster and achieve more,* not as a means by which we go over old ground, slow things down and frustrate part, if not all, of our audience. Pre-reading should enable a higher quality discussion, more scrutiny, better questions, more effective analysis and a more holistic, considered, successful outcome. A simple strategy that I encourage my clients to consider is to review their pre-reading, its use and the results that are achieved. If it's not achieving what I have outlined above, then the time is long past where it should be changed. Of course, the exact same goes for face-to-face meetings I should say.

Get The Number Of Attendees Right

Here too we encountered challenges. Just how many people should we ask to our remote meetings? Having too many people invited to a meeting, often without a clear understanding of why they are there, is one of the most common mistakes I observed. A typical example of where this occurs often is with a project team or horizontal leadership group which meets regularly around the same issue, account or project.

The question I pose is an interesting one because there is some research that supports the fact that both *the size* of the group and *the seniority of attendees* will impact the degree of 'group think' that evolves, unless we actively plan and manage against it. For example, if the goal of a remote meeting is to make a decision, there is research[28] which suggests that conformity increases along with the number of people in an audience. Solomon Asch was a psychologist who conducted some famous research back in the 1950s which was designed to explore the effects of group pressure on our judgement and decision making. In essence, what he found was that conformity rose when the number of people in a group rose. Once the group exceeded five in number, then the amount of conformity didn't change significantly beyond that.

In addition, Asch[28] also found that conformity tends to rise with attendees who are more senior in stature. He also showed that there is a perception of more power or influence or expertise with such individuals, and as a result, there tends to be greater alignment with their perspective. Both my observed sessions and interviews, perhaps unsurprisingly, support this research.

Laura Stack[29] quotes Bob Fritsch and Josh Peck from Bloomberg who recommend the following:

- If the purpose of our meeting is to share information, in other words a cascade of information that the audience needs to understand, then the number of people joining the call is not limited. My caveat to this recommendation is (a) length of message (b) whether we ask the audience to put the camera on – to which I always say 'yes' (c) *carefully reflect* on whether another media would be more effective e.g. a podcast.
- If the purpose of the meeting is to brainstorm, then between twenty to thirty-five people are recommended. My research would suggest that this is on the high side. I did not observe a single instance where a group over twenty was effective in in terms of ensuring an equal balance of high-quality contribution across the board.
- If the purpose of the meeting is to have a discussion, then fewer than twenty are recommended.
- If the purpose of the meeting is to get agreement or alignment, then between six and fourteen people are recommended.
- If the purpose of the meeting is to make a decision, then between three to six leaders are recommended.
- If the purpose of the meeting is to plan actions, then twenty-five to forty are recommended. Again, my research reflected something different to this. Above twenty is very high and I personally would recommend that even this number represents a challenge when it comes to staying on track and on task.

Do Our Homework In Relation To Our Stakeholders

During our working day, how often do we find ourselves almost bouncing from one conference call or telepresence to another? There are many occasions during which I have worked with clients who are literally *back-to-back on their calendar* from the start of the day until its end. So, when suggesting to 'do your homework', I do not wish to appear trite. This is great in theory, but much harder to do in reality, and failure to do so is a high-risk strategy.

To be clear, I am *not* talking about preparing material in relation to the content for the meeting. Usually professionals do – although we've all experienced the consequences of those who have not. That's generally a given. What *I am* talking about is preparing carefully for the following:

- What are the 'top of mind' objectives, key priorities and challenges for our audience on the call which they are looking to deliver? Everyone has key performance indicators that they need to drive through others, so everything to which they support or offer practical commitment will be connected to successful execution against these priorities. Such goals might be weekly, monthly, quarterly or yearly, but irrespective of the industry and part of the value chain that our stakeholders represent, we need to know what these are and connect our issues clearly to their priorities.

- What are their preferences around *how we communicate* to our audience? Do we know what these are? Are we capable of being able to flex our approach to more closely match theirs?

- How much *rehearsal of what we need to say* have we done? This might be unexpected to read; however, there is an enormous difference between the cognitive processes that enable us to identify what we plan to say *and then the mechanical activity of actually saying it.* When the spotlight is on us and we know the whole audience is listening and looking at us, it's important to be crisp, clear and compelling. That requires practice, both to build muscle memory, but also to refine our message and to build confidence in our ability to convey it under pressure. If we add into the mix the notion of the stakes being high, because our message might be contentious, or our ask might be the culmination of three months working flat out 24/7, then it matters what the response is that we elicit and that means we'll have some degree of performance anxiety around it.

- Who do we need to get onside in advance of the meeting? Especially if our recommendations are going to particularly impact their team? Or, if what we're asking for is quite a lot in relation to their budget, their time, their people? Or, if what we're asking for is going to directly impact their objectives? Creating a groundswell of support which culminates in aligning with what we suggest doesn't always happen with one pitch. It requires strategy and the necessity of working with people individually to understand their issues and concerns, as well as what they need to see and hear in order to support what we are recommending. This takes time, patience and a strategy.

- Finally, always remember the cardinal rule – *no surprises.* Otherwise we deserve what we will get.

My research revealed that these areas are not always fully considered, let alone prepared for, properly. All too often, professionals fail to quickly and effectively connect with their audience, reduce the tension that is inevitable at the beginning of the conversation and increase rapport as the meeting progresses. From such a position, we are almost doomed to fail. To be candid, we should be preparing for interactions with our colleagues anyway, irrespective of whether or not we're in the same room as colleagues, but the simple truth is this:

- If we don't understand what our stakeholders are doing, what we're asking for, what we're talking about in terms of how it relates to our audience, their teams and their priorities, then *they don't care about it.* In other words, if we get the 'what' wrong in our communication, then we will fail to engage them.
- If we don't flex our style to our audience quickly, then for different reasons, they will stop listening to the message. This communication style challenge is *instrumental* in helping to build rapport or conversely, to destroy trust. We all have preferences around pace, content, cadence, focus areas when we speak and are going to be more influenced by those who are 'talking our language' – literally. So, if we get the 'how' wrong in our communication, then again, we will fail to connect.
- If we do not *rehearse* our key messages in advance, and rely solely on our cognitive thinking processes, then unless we already have a rich level of capability we will also fail. Why? Because how we *think* about key messages and stories that we wish to convey requires cognitive skills. However how we *communicate* key messages and stories requires mechanical skills. This is a completely different process from what we think about saying.
- If we don't get key stakeholders onside in advance, then we should prepare for a potentially meeting ending rejection of our request.

- If we do not create and execute a communication campaign in order to build support, overcome objections and create agreement and alignment, then it's an extremely tall order to get approval if what we are asking for is heard for the first time, in a group, with significant impacts for attendees. As a strategy, is simply will not work.

Understand The Audience Behaviour We Might Face

- Let's begin by exploring the reality of the audience we face. Whenever we dial into a T-con, join a telepresence or have a telephone conversation, we will face specific, and very different, potential audience behaviours. By the way, these also apply to face-to-face scenarios such as team meetings, client case conferences, seminars, workshops and the like. Our challenge is in being able to both recognise the different types of audience, as well as then being able to flex our communication style to be able to handle it and bring the individuals on side. How many of the following individuals have you met on a remote call?

- **The Tourist:** This audience member is metaphorically on holiday. By joining our virtual meeting, they are away from their colleagues, their boss, their customers, their inbox, their to-do list and are delighted by the prospect. They don't necessarily care about the content of the conversation or remote meeting, they are, by default, *not doing something else* that they do not enjoy or want to do. They have a break, an escape, and the opportunity for a mini holiday by being on our call. Perhaps they have a great cup of coffee and a biscuit in front of them and they are simply going to kick back, relax and have a good time.

- **The Hostage:** As the name would suggest, they don't want to be there. They don't care about the content of the meeting; they don't want to know what we're talking about because they are simply not interested. They have other places to be and other things they would much rather be doing. Indeed, they might have tried to get out of the meeting but been gently encouraged, or overtly mandated, to attend. Perhaps they have to be there because it would be politically inappropriate to be absent. It's a hostage situation because there are a hundred other places they would rather be, and a hundred other things they would rather do, and yet here they are here, on our call, t-con or telepresence.

- **The Explorer:** Is someone who is neither of the two audience types above. They are open and neutral to the meeting in front of them. They are willing to engage and explore the content to see what value it will have for them, their team and stakeholders. They are *not* a 'soft touch'; they can be alienated and become disengaged if we don't create value in the quality of the conversation, and its relevance to their needs.
- **The Terrorist:** Not a common audience type, but one nevertheless that we can meet. Obviously, they are out to cause trouble. Their reasons for so doing might be connected to our topic or, may have nothing to do with it. However, no matter, they are on our call, they are not happy, they are in the mood for conflict and out to create it. The purpose of their attending is to create a stir and we need to look out because it is certain that they will do so.

Get Our Friends Lined Up To Support Us

So, picture the scene. We are going to pitch an idea and know already that most, some, all of the audience will be opposed to it. I very recently worked with a client who was challenged with this exact scenario, and he was attempting to drive a $5m process change within the organisation. Whilst there were many things that we did to change his story, make his message more concise and compelling and enhance his delivery, *the most important thing we did* was help him to deploy a strategy to build support and consensus ahead of the meeting. This was more than just benign head nodding; it was persuading stakeholders to agree with his proposal *and,* who were willing to support his pitch and join the call. In global, matrix businesses we have multiple internal and external stakeholders and often, driving change is difficult and frustrating. However, if we get support from the right influencers and involve them in our campaign to create change, it will make a profound difference in the face of strong resistance. Remember, this is a remote environment and the trust levels are low and bar set to persuade others very high and so it couldn't be more difficult. We must strategise to have advocates who are willing to support us on the call.

Managing The Internal And External Meeting Attendee

How often do we find ourselves in meetings with our colleagues and customers? In a sales environment, probably 'quite often' is the answer. What I have observed is the difference between those meetings where there was clear alignment and preparation in advance, causing the meeting to go well and be completed efficiently, versus those occasions where clearly this was lacking. If it's our meeting, what we need to be joined up. Let's be clear, if we've organised the call, our colleagues will leave it to us to have figured out, and if we don't, are unlikely to immediately jump to our defence. It's not because we can't trust them, it's because *it's our meeting*. So, let's take the lead. What's our (as the internal team) objective? Who do we need to be on the call? What's their role? What do we want? What don't we want? What's our fallback position? Where do we want to spend time? Where don't we want to spend time? How can we leverage the value of everyone we've invited to join? Who's covering which topics? What are the no-go discussion areas? How will we handle issues X, Y and Z? Clarity and strategy are required here, as well as continual review if this is a call that happens regularly. Influence doesn't happen by invitation; it happens when we step into the space and take the lead. That's when we can convey impact, presence and leadership.

Now take those questions and apply them to the ladies and gentlemen who are represent the client. I have had a conversation with a client only this week who commented that they had five people from different departments on the call, whilst the client had just one person attending. That's almost intimidation! It is our responsibility to make this work for both parties, and this type of incident I have seen happen *repeatedly with different clients*. It shows we haven't done the right kind of advance preparation to ensure meeting success and it's our responsibility to learn and change moving forward. If we do not, our remote meetings develop a brand for being not that interesting or useful, generally seen as a chance to dial in and tune out and as a result, engagement drops and so does our remote impact. We have to get this right.

Decide On Our Influencing Strategy

The fundamental reason we're on the call or joining the telepresence is because we want to influence. Isn't it? Whilst I understand that we may want to learn in more depth about a specific situation, project or problem, we're not doing so simply for the sake of it. Or at least, we shouldn't be. Far too often we can experience individuals who join a virtual call or meeting and say nothing. What's the point of them being there? Seriously? Perhaps sometimes that has been us in the past? If we're going to make time to attend a t-con or telepresence, then we must want to influence the discussion. An aside; if we don't want to influence it then don't bother attending and just ask someone to send over the notes. I'm serious. So, in addition to the homework that we need to do in order to better understand our stakeholders, we then need to decide *which strategy to influence* we are going to adopt.

If we understand our stakeholders and colleagues well, and we know to which approach they will respond best, then obviously the outcome we will drive is more likely to be successful for us. If we don't think about it and have never considered it then we still might be successful, but it will be due to more luck than judgement. I have outlined below some strategies to *deliberately adopt* in order to drive the result we want through our approach to influencing others. Obviously, they work in both the remote and the face-to-face environment. Robert Cialdini, in his excellent book *'Persuasion'[14],* suggests that there are six primary ways in which we can influence others. The distinctions explained below are based on his excellent research.

Persuasion Through Logic

It does exactly what it says on the tin. Influencing others through the power of logic. By the way and for the purposes of clarity, logic is defined as making a series of statements, each one of which must be true if what has preceded it is also true. For example: "we know that it gets dark at 4pm in winter and that our challenge is to create solar powered lighting that works throughout the evening. The testing of our beta product reveals that it captures light during the daytime very effectively and can power up the battery with enough energy to illuminate for sixteen hours. Our tests also show that the batteries lose power very quickly once activated by the lack of light. So, we have to look at the components of the batteries to see what is causing the power drain". Persuasion through logic is a powerful influencing strategy that is used globally in almost every culture. It remains highly effective.

Asserting

This is simply the strategy of stating what we believe or want in any situation. As an approach, this can be highly effective *if executed correctly.* In other words, we need to *feel* self-confident *and we need to convey it.* How we communicate non-verbally, if we can be seen, and how we sound, especially in relation to our tone of voice, speed of delivery, use of pause and whether or not we upward inflect at the end of sentences all play a very significant part in the success of this approach. For example: "I believe we can hit the aggressive sales target for quarter three, and I am certain that you will all succeed too if you agree with my recommendation". This is an assertion. However, a word of warning, overuse can work against us and we can be accused of being heavy handed, or conveying confidence but no substance, or be seen as being very unyielding to the perspective of others.

Negotiating

This is not the formal end-to-end process to secure a deal that I am referring to here. Instead, we are talking about how to trade with each other for co-operation. This has the most impact when it is used implicitly rather explicitly, because the latter can feel very manipulative and almost grubby. It reeks of 'if you scratch my back and I'll scratch yours'. I prefer to view it as a strategy that is about finding wins for both parties. How we can make it work authentically is by doing our homework regarding our stakeholders key metrics, priorities and top of mind issues and finding connections to us in two very specific ways: (a) how we can help them in the achievement of their issues (b) identify the ways in which by helping them, it helps us too. Language such as "I think there's an opportunity for both of us here", or "my goal is to make it work for everybody" works because it makes clear our intent, the concept of a win/win is universally understood and appealing, plus it's a chance for our stakeholder to feel good about themselves *in helping us too.*

Legitimising

This influencing strategy is focused around appealing to authority. To adopt a legitimising strategy means to that we are declaring our approach to be right because of another person or group that is deemed to have greater authority. The most obvious ones include "this isn't my idea; this is what my boss says we must do". The advantage of this approach is that it can drive compliance and speed of response. However, from a standpoint of presence I personally dislike and discourage it. Why?

Because it communicates that we have no personal power in the discussion and that we are relying on the perceived positional power of others to drive a result. It says: 'it's not me' and also 'I can't do anything' and who would want to be perceived in such a way? Secondly it conveys no personal responsibility or ownership in this situation. Sometimes as leaders we need to communicate a decision we don't like or don't agree with. In any event we still need to own it. My view regarding this approach is that we may as well stick a post-it note on our forehead and say 'I can't influence anyone about anything'. Best avoided.

Appealing To A Relationship

This influencing strategy is about driving support with people who are well known to us and with whom we have a good relationship. It is definitely an effective strategy and research would suggest that it is used globally to great effect. For example: "Bob, you and I go back a long way and you know that I would never suggest an approach that goes against what you believe. I know this is absolutely the best decision and I am saying unequivocally as a friend and long-standing colleague that it does not compromise those values which you hold dear".

Socialising

This approach is about getting to know others and being friendly. It involves both a strategic and a tactical component. For example, in the longer term is does mean investing time to get to know others, create relationships and build connection with the person, not just the professional. So, this means making time to get to know people and talk about things in addition to work. In tactical terms, it means investing time to do the 'non work chat' when we meet remotely.

Bring Solutions, Ideas And Alignment To The Meeting

I work with a client in the digital sector. One leader whom I have had the pleasure of partnering with for a while had some great ideas about how to convert a legacy office site into a space for some high potential talent training, including hackathons, graduate onboarding events, client networking seminars amongst other things. His frustration was that these great ideas were going nowhere fast. He has lots of energy as a leader and the concept was a good one, but momentum around getting practical and financial support from within the business was progressing at a *snail's pace.* Here's the point: driving change within a business isn't easy at the best of times. However, if we are going to sell an idea for change successfully, whether it's on a remote call or face-to-face, then we are far more likely to make serious progress when we ask for help *with ideas, alignment and solution already lined up.* So, getting the support of teams who would need to be involved in making the change happen, creating sequential steps to demonstrate progress and business value lined up, having ideas at hand to address some of the most predictable concerns and issues of our stakeholders; if all of this activity done is done in advance of the meeting, it will make our progress *much more speedy and successful.*

Learn From Our Mistakes

No judgement here, but the reality is that we all make them. When *we know* our remote meeting didn't work, then we should park our ego at the door, embrace the opportunity to have yet more impact and learn from what didn't work.

And Finally – Is This The Right Tool For The Job?

Be honest – is this the best media through which to communicate? Dependent on the topic, audience, our objective, our culture and our brand, we need to reflect on whether or not a remote meeting is the right way forward. Should it be face to face? Should it be 1:1 rather than 1: many? Should it via a podcast? A live stream with Q&A? Direct messaging? An email? Should we be communicating the message, or should we ask others in our organisation to convey it? Always, always, always reflect on what is the best media for the message. We have so many tools at our disposal to communicate remotely and we should be rigorous and ruthless in evaluating the best remote media tool for the job on a regular basis.

Chapter Seven – Starting Well

A Word Or Two About This Content

As this chapter unfolds, it will be immediately apparent that every strategy that we explore can be used in a face-to-face environment as well as a virtual one. I am not suggesting that any of these approaches *only work* in the remote meeting scenario – far from it. What *I am saying* is two key things. Firstly, it's important to remember that in the remote meeting environment, often the visual and the non-verbal tools from our influencing toolbox are missing. If the camera is turned off, then getting it right verbally *is the only way* to have presence and impact. Secondly, during the three years which I took to research this book, what became very clear was that the following verbal strategies take on *a far greater significance* remotely. These strategies are *really important to do well remotely.* They relate deeply to the way in which humans build trust with each other, and how that is challenged when talking to screens. The additional benefit is that we can also apply these skills and strategies to a variety of other situations, as we can for a lot of content about which I write. So, sit back, relax and read on.

Right Before The Meeting Starts

There are some things we must do in order to show that we're prepared and the more we conduct our business remotely, the easier it is to become a little too relaxed on these steps. All too often, I have joined calls where people are late because they didn't download the latest software update, they've lost their headset, their keyboard has run out of battery etc. etc. etc. It sounds daft; but is more common that we might like to admit. Therefore, some tips to ensure that we get it right, right before the meeting starts including:

- Ensure the latest version of the software for our meeting platform is loaded; including any updates.
- Check that we have back up batteries if using remote keyboards or mousepads, just in case they die in the middle of a really important presentation to a key client. Been there; done that.
- Test our headset and if we don't have one; invest in one, as well as camera and audio levels.

84

- Offer to open the call fifteen minutes early and be there to resolve any technology issues. This is preferable to wasting fifteen minutes at the top of the call dealing with 'Bob', who can't plug his headset in, find his email invite etc.
- Turn our camera on and ask others to do the same if it's our meeting, go on mute and come off it to welcome others, open up the 'chat' function.
- Put a welcome note in the chat function and the pre-reading as a handy reference for anyone who's forgotten to read it.

Small things all of them; but cumulatively they have a big impact and trust me, I have seen meetings take a very bad turn through not paying attention to one or more of the above.

The Concept of 'Micro Moments'

Conveying presence, or our brand, often happens in what I term 'micro moments'. Bear with me. The world of work today means that we are operating at warp speed, across times zones and matrix structures where we don't have the same opportunity to build trusted relationships in the way that we would if we were all working in the same office and saw each other every day. We live in this two or three screen (or more!) society where too many professionals are overly fascinated with their devices, appear distracted and hence aren't listening properly most of the time. What all of this means is that all too often, we join virtual calls and meetings where we have a small amount of time and a small number of occasions in which to communicate effectively and have impact.

If we don't understand how to make the most of these moments, then we certainly run the risk of being forgettable. Or, we lose our audience for good and are remembered only for not being persuasive. Most professionals don't realise that the moment has passed, but they do recognise when the conversation isn't going the way they would like, or when they have not achieved the desired outcome from the discussion. However, if we take advantage of these micro moments, either as the owner of the meeting or the attendee, then it makes a significant difference to our ability to be successful.

We're Judged By Our 'Hello'

There is a well-known film called '*Jerry* McGuire[19], starring Tom Cruise as a sports agent who has a moral epiphany, gets fired, loses all his client bar one, and if that wasn't bad enough, experiences something of a meltdown in his personal life. Just as things seem to hit rock bottom, and in a last-ditch attempt to salvage his relationship, he goes to see his partner, Renée Zellweger, and launches into a lengthy speech to try to win her back. She retorts with one of the most memorable lines in cinematic history. It is quite simply: "you had me at hello". Cue the music, a passionate reconciliation and the rest, as they say, is history.

Whilst the line itself is not quite in the Lauren and Bacall stratosphere of movie classic zingers, it caught the imagination of the movie-going public, and with good reason. Research suggests that there is more to the line that we might imagine. According to studies conducted by Princeton and the University of Glasgow[20], we judge others within *half a second* of hearing their voice, and without seeing what the person looks like. Seriously, that's all it takes. The team recorded sixty-four men and women reading a passage of text and then simply extracted the word 'hello'. As a result, these one-word recordings were played to more than three hundred students who were asked to rate the voices according to specific characteristics, including dominance, likeability, worthiness and trustworthiness.

So, what do we infer from simply one word? It would seem that there are some fascinating gender differences, including the facts that men were judged to be more trustworthy if they were slightly higher pitched than average, whilst women were thought to be more dependable if they lowered their vocal tone towards the end of a word. In addition, for both men and women, if they communicated a vocal tone that sounded more resonant, then the impression that they gave was one of dominance.

The most fascinating part of the research suggests that *almost all* of the three hundred and twenty students who took part in the study had noted the same first impressions. It would appear that that our ability to make rapid judgments of other people is part of a fundamental survival mechanism. As humans, we form rapid, instinctive opinions of others, based on very small pieces of verbal data and create impressions of others in terms of their trustworthiness and dominance. This is not a conscious decision, it's instinctive and what is *so fascinating* is the consistency with which *we all do it.*

To Introduce Or Not To Introduce?

Beware of wasting too much time on introductions if the group size is veering towards too big. What represents too big? Well if you're heading up towards ten attendees then there's a real danger that a disproportionate amount of time can be taken up with introductions. I joined one call of ten attendees where the average introduction time was two minutes per person. We can all do that maths, and this is far too much time to be spent on 'who's who'.

If we want to facilitate introductions, there are a couple of ways to do so:

- **Set the ground rules:** around what we want people to share by way of introduction. By way of example, their name, role on the project and key areas of responsibilities. Obviously there are many alternatives, and in any event, a maximum of three things to say that's for certain. I timed one introduction during my research which lasted almost five minutes. That is an eye-watering amount of time and an unnecessary waste of it.
- **Introduce Others For Them:** This requires us to do our homework and we need to be concise; but it's a very effective way of staying in control, managing the group and getting going with the nitty gritty more quickly.
- **Send An Introduction Email In Advance:** To provide this core information in one note. Again, an efficient way to get going quickly.

The High Impact Introduction

If we are going to introduce ourselves, either as the person who is running the remote meeting, or as the person attending it, we must remember that this is another example of a micro moment. For anyone who has ever been on a training course, we know that one of the first activities as a delegate that we are invited to do is introduce ourselves. We've barely sat down, worked out whether or not we'll need our glasses to read the screen and sipped our coffee before this particular ritual begins. As a trainer often running such workshops, I can almost hear the collective sigh and see from the front of the room the general eye rolling and shoulder slump as people are asked to complete the request. No one usually wants to go first and when finally, a delegate volunteers, what happens? Typically, there follows a set of slightly stilted, embarrassed and almost apologetic introductions that are *utterly underwhelming.* Now my questions as a trainer are many, starting with: why is that? Why do we fail to prepare for the first, public, verbal demonstration of our brand? Why does it feel so tense and awkward? And, if we feel this way in a face-to-face environment, what do we think it's going to be like when we are trying to do this remotely?

Introducing ourselves isn't exclusively the domain of a training course. Whether it's at the beginning of conference calls, going to a pitch or attending a client meeting, there is regularly and invariably a requirement to let the audience know who we are, what we're doing and most importantly, why the rest of us should care. The 'high impact introduction' is one of those *career long capabilities* that we will be called upon repeatedly to execute over the years in a wide variety of situations. It's an opportunity to create a positive, impressive connection to the audience that starts to reduce tension and increase rapport.

However, too many times what we hear from others is either (a) weapons grade waffle that goes on until the end of time or (b) a stilted, quiet, embarrassed, quick comment that absolutely does not inspire anyone or (c) it just sounds 'blah'. The other phenomenon that regularly occurs is herd mentality, where we copy the format of the first person who spoke (how original!), irrespective of whether or not their introduction was any good.

So, as you may have discerned, I have some energy around this topic, and given that this chapter is all about interventions with impact, it is essential to ensure that our first contribution is impressive and persuasive. The best way to do that is to take the opportunity to tell a story. To be clear, when I use the word 'story', I don't mean an anecdote (e.g. there was an Italian, a Frenchman and an Englishman who walked into a pub......). It's not that kind of approach. A story is a structured message designed to influence and inspire others. It's not a lengthy narrative. Our goal through a high impact introduction is to convey a message that engages and intrigues the audience. This means:

1. **Split our introduction into three parts**. The power of the number three is enormous because as part of our survival mechanism, we look for rhythm and pattern. We all know that stories have a beginning, middle and end and this means that there is a logical flow to what we are saying. So, as just one of

many examples, when thinking about our introduction, it could be structured as follows:

- o Who We Are
- o Why We Are There
- o What Our Goal Is For The Discussion (in terms of what others care about)

This is only one example, as there are many different narrative structures that you could use. Trust me, there plenty to choose from and an alternative might be:

- o The Past (what we've done before)
- o The Present (what we're doing now)
- o The Future (where we're headed next)
- Or,
  - o What We Do Now
  - o Why We're Here
  - o What We're Looking Forward To

The point is to get the narrative structure right first, and it makes all the difference to the quality and quantity of what we say.

2. **Have different versions for different situations.** High impact communication means having different versions for our introduction for different audiences and allows us to communicate in the right context. Our ability to convey credibility will be judged by the audience, so it pays to have a number in reserve that are well rehearsed and ready to use when we need it.

3. **Use metaphor and analogy.** This can work really well when explaining something that might be complex, dry or dull plus, it has the key advantage of being remembered and repeated. This can be particularly helpful if we have a job title or role that either no one understands or, by nature of the role, there are a range of pre-conceptions and misconceptions about it. For this think 'tax inspector', 'estate agent' etc. And to be clear, I have nothing but respect for every single profession, my point is that it's about awareness of bias as well as appreciation of our audience. Some roles will need more clarity, others will not.

4. **Look and sound like we are glad to be there.** All too often we appear uncomfortable, somewhat tense and slightly awkward, whilst also being desperately keen to get the whole thing over with. Social tension is at its highest at the beginning of meeting and rapport is at its lowest. Our first contribution is an essential opportunity to lower the tension and increase the rapport. We can do so if we use energy, pace, smile, look at our audience and relax when we speak. Remember in a remote environment I always encourage the audience to put their cameras on!

5. **Be brief.** Knowing when to stop talking is *essential.* Much as I get frustrated with introductions that are too short, it's also the case that endless waffling isn't a good idea either. I have a client who was specifically asked to work with me because he didn't know when to stop talking and worse, he did not realise it. His introduction was the first place that we worked hard to address, because if this isn't right, everything that follows it is under serious threat.

6. **Don't underestimate the need to rehearse.** The thing about communication is that intellectually it is not difficult to understand. The trick comes in the delivery. How we mentally process information is *a million miles away* from how the words come out of our mouths. So, we should record our introduction on our phone or computer and practise in front of the mirror so that we can see how we might look to others.

Warming Up The Room

At the top of this chapter, I talk about the fact that social tension is high, and rapport is low at the beginning of any human interaction. This is true whether or not we are meeting remotely with people we have known for years, or whether we are connecting for the first time. The question is why? Quite simply it is connected with the fact that as human beings, our *survival mechanism* kicks in. In any human interaction, we all have the same aim; namely *to leave that interaction with our sense of self-worth intact.* As a result, at the start of communicating with others, we are all trying to work out if we will be 'okay' in this space. Specific strategies to do this are coming momentarily in this chapter, but before I outline them, there is a critical backdrop to the strategies which I will explain.

Investing In The 'Emotional Bank Account' Of Others

Steven Covey writes about the concept of 'the emotional bank account' in his book *Seven Habits For Highly Effective People*[17]. He explores how trust is built between human beings interacting with each other, using the metaphor of a bank account. When we make deposits, the level of rapport increases, and when we make withdrawals, the level of rapport reduces. Whether the context is the duration of a remote meeting, or whether it is over time and the development of a relationship, what makes the difference to trust levels is the extent to which we have invested in others' emotional bank account over time.

It is also worth pointing out that at the beginning of an interaction and for the first interaction of the day, the metaphorical bank balance is set back to zero. So even when it is someone who we know well and like and respect, we need to be mindful to make deposits in order to grow rapport *in that moment* and throughout that interaction.

Strategies Which Work

There are a number that are extremely effective to reach our audience and make a connection. As always, I'm a fan of choice, and equally, it's when and how they are deployed that will determine whether or not we have people on side or whether they have switched off. So be curious, be open to experimentation and be willing to pay attention to the impact that these approaches have after the event.

Small Talk

This is *such* an important skill to master and has particular relevance in the context of communicating remotely. Think about it for a moment. Remember that we are not in the same room physically, and so as a result, don't have the opportunity to experience the three-dimensional, literal, physical presence of others. We may be on a slight time delay, reliant on the quality of our broadband connection, all of which merely adds to the difficulty and complexity of creating a smooth ebb and flow in the conversation. We underestimate the impact of small talk to building an easy rapport. If the scenario is a remote meeting where we can't see others and have only our voice to work with, then the difficulty rapidly increases. All of these things dramatically impact our ability to read our audience accurately and gauge what is going on. We are missing crucial cues from which to infer our environment and be able to adjust correctly to it. We know that social tension is at its highest at the beginning of an interaction, and rapport is at its lowest. However, we still need to break the ice – even when talking to people we know and like – at the top of the call.

In the past few months, I have been working with several clients in the professional services area of late, where one might think that confident, bright, successful professionals will have the capability to do small talk well extremely well. The reality is simply not the case. I was talking with a group of lawyers only recently who spoke about the difficulties which they have, and in which they particularly observe others, including more senior colleagues, at the very beginning of a call.

Picture the scene.

We dial into a telepresence or t-con in a professionally prompt fashion only to find a very senior stakeholder, or that one person in the team who is perceived as challenging on the client side. Or, maybe it's neither of these scenarios, it's just one or two other people only on the call, and we are faced with the challenge of what to say. My clients spoke of the awkwardness and tension experienced in these moments and the challenge of knowing what to do. One talked of her senior partner actually saying: "let's all go on mute and get something useful done before the client joins".

Just think about that for a moment.

Small talk isn't about tasks; it's about relationships. Small talk is a building block to creating better, more meaningful connections with others so that we can collaborate, co-operate and co-exist with clients and colleagues far more effectively. It's a mechanism that helps to build trust, and with trust comes the opportunity to influence others. All too often there is the easy and lazy excuse of using this time as an opportunity to do exactly what the senior partner in the earlier example indicated. Cue for all of us to revert back to emails and start tapping away. *I'm not talking about wasting a lot of time.* I'm not talking about wittering away for hours. What I'm talking about is making a connection; changing the nature of the relationship; getting to know the person behind the screen.

The challenge then becomes: 'what to say'? I use an acronym with my clients called WIFE and it helps enormously.

W – stands for 'weather'. Look, I'm proudly British and this is a national sport. We can talk about the weather until the end of time. In fairness, with the amount of travel I do, there are a number of countries around the world that do what I would call 'big weather'. The point is that everyone experiences it, most people have an opinion on it and it's a very easy, unrehearsed topic about which to speak.

I – stands for 'interests'. This is not about pretending to be interested in something that we're not, but rather it's about knowing a little about a number of different things. And of course, it's an opportunity to talk about something that you are interested in, or even more effectively, find out what others are interested in and ask questions about that.

F – stands for 'family'. Everyone belongs to a family of one sort or another – pets, friends, godchildren, distant relatives all count.

E – stands for 'events'. At the time of writing this book, we are in the middle of the covid19 crisis. There is little talk of anything else. However, beyond it, any event large or small is covered within this category.

All too often in business, and my research bears this out, there is little or no small talk, we go on mute to crank out those emails until the very last second, and then start the meeting. However, we then wonder why we aren't getting the traction and aren't making the progress that we would like with our priorities. Part of the reason is because quite simply, we're not building the relationship and investing in the emotional bank account of others. We can *definitely do that* in a couple of minutes of indulging in small talk – it's that powerful. To be clear, I'm not suggesting that it's just about small talk and I'm not saying that we should take the first fifteen minutes of a call to do small talk. What I *am* suggesting is that before a meeting starts, these short windows of time represent a micro moment in which to convey your brand, have impact and start to build a different type of trust and connection with others on the call. Small talk is a skill and a strength to build for all of us.

The Scene Setter

A highly effective strategy at the beginning a meeting that we *absolutely have to use* is the scene setter. In other words, we need to let our audience know what they can expect, how we will engage with them and, most importantly, what's the value for our audience of the interaction we are about to have. I call this 'the three Ps'. By the way, this strategy is not only confined to remote communication. I have spoken about this in a previous chapter, because it can be used to make our email invitations much more compelling. We can also use it at the beginning of a face-to-face conversation, a sales call, an interview, a presentation, a training workshop, a review, an appraisal, a team meeting and in fact *any other situation that calls for us to talk to others.* In fact, its impact is so great that we can use it in the written form as well.

I unapologetically refer to it again here, because it should also be used to set the scene at the beginning of a remote meeting. 'The three Ps' represent the 'purpose, process and payoff'. So, in a remote context and by way of example, we might find ourselves needing to pitch out an idea to our colleagues, offer some recommendations to our senior leaders, look to secure financial support from our global horizontal team or sell something new to our customers. By so doing, using 'the three Ps', we want to explain the following:

- **Purpose** – this means the objective of the conversation. It needs to explain the outcome to be achieved *and is not the same* as an agenda. Think of it as the purpose being the destination and the agenda is the route map to get us there. For example, *"we need to make a final decision regarding the proposed expansion of our manufacturing division of the business into the Asia-Pacific region".*

- **Process** – this means the way that we will engage during this interaction. So, for example, imagine that we are pitching some slides to colleagues on a telepresence. We might say for the 'process' part something such as *"I have 3 slides to share with you and I am certain that you will all have questions. If you can hold off asking those questions until the end, then I can take them once you've heard the full story'.* Or, as an alternative, *"I have three slides and you will have questions, so, feel free to ask them throughout the course of our time together on the call today".* These are just illustrative. There are many other examples to explain the 'process' part of the conversation, however the point is: we let our audience know *how* to engage with us right from the start. This is a crucial component of our communication as a scene setter at the beginning of an interaction, because social tension at this point is at its highest and rapport is at its lowest. This holds true whether we know our audience really well, or whether they are individuals who are as good as unknown to us. By taking the lead with this 'process' information, what we are doing is informing our colleagues what to expect and how to participate in this group setting. It's essential because survival is an essential facet of our existence as human beings. Of course this is not a life or death situation, but it is certainly a survival situation in which our need to save face, be seen to have value and be worthy of respect/admiration etc. from our peers and to feel good about ourselves within this interaction are all readily to the fore. In addition, within the 'process' part of the message it is essential to explain the etiquette during the call (e.g. cameras on, microphone on mute, use of chat function, hand up etc.) If we do not, there will be confusion and a myriad of ways that the audience will, or won't, engage with the conversation. When we review this section, we might think 'there's a lot to say'. However, if we rehearse and are fluent, then it doesn't take long *at all,* and has a dramatic impact in terms of keeping the engagement levels high on the call.

- **Payoff** – this means the benefit of what is about to happen. So, again, using the example above it might be *"we will be clear on how this project can add value to each of our teams and also feel comfortable about what is and is not included within the final remit".*

What makes this verbal contribution so powerful is that all too often none, or only some, of this is explained. We fail to set the tone, take control, be clear and concise right from the beginning and as a result, the audience simply does not understand what's really happening. The consequences are significant at many levels.

- Our audience will easily and readily disengage because they don't know and don't care about the session and turn to their emails to start cranking those out instead.
- At an operational level these conversations are simply inefficient because there are lots of people on conference calls and telepresence meetings who are not really listening to each other. We are inefficient not only with our time but also with our understanding because we weren't really listening and weren't engaged properly.
- Strategically, the decisions around which these sessions are organised take longer to be reached, or alternatively they get paused part way through the

discussion and deferred. Everything slows down and erodes value. As a business we are less agile, less profitable because of the waste in this process, less responsive and less able to flex to the requirements of the business and our customers. It also impacts employee engagement. This is why meetings have such a poor brand reputation.

How do we know this is happening in our world? Simply ask yourself by reviewing your calendar how often in the last two weeks you have been invited to or attended virtual meetings and calls that didn't add value. For too many professionals in too many organisations this is simply happening far too often.

Use Their Names

It's the first sound that we all learn that has profound meaning for us. It may not be the first thing we say, but when others use our names, our attention and connection dramatically rises. If we are hosting a meeting and don't know everyone well who is on the call, then it has additional value to use their name. So, not only as part of interacting with them right at the beginning, but also as part of updating new joiners to the call as to who has already dialled in, and it's a great way to start warming up the room. Why? Because it's public recognition, which again, from childhood, is something that we all love. This strategy also has other benefits as well. For the host, it gives us the opportunity to reinforce the names of attendees to lock them into our short-term memory, and in addition, it's also an excellent strategy for retaining engagement because we are using a public recognition strategy to engage others. We will always be invested in understanding how we are referenced during a conversation.

Demonstrate Courtesy

Sound old-fashioned? Far from it. We live in a world that *craves* more civility[38] with a significant cost to business where incivility exists. The fast paced, distracted, technology driven world in which we all live has eroded our capacity to make the time to show courtesy to others. We were taught as children about the importance of good manners and their erosion over time has been significant. Remember, in the remote environment we have taken away a number of the mechanisms which counterbalance being less civil (i.e. we might not be seen on camera, we're not in the same physical space to read micro cues etc.) So, it remains true that saying things such as 'please' and 'thank-you' help reduce tension and increase rapport, it's an investment in the emotional bank account of others and so we should use them in a relevant, authentic way.

Show Appreciation

Who reading this right now is thinking 'I have so much appreciation shown to me in my life that I *couldn't possibly* require any more?' Absolutely nobody that I know. A nuance to courtesy, this is a strategy which allows us to invest in the emotional bank account of someone who, by way of example (a) might have joined the call at 6am local time (b) rearranged their day and priorities to accommodate this remote meeting at short notice (c) has pulled together a ton of work for us to make the call work etc. The point is that by showing that we've noticed, and we *genuinely appreciate their efforts* means that we are making up ground in the relationship on what might otherwise be silent fury, growing resentment or a sense of resignation towards us. This isn't often admitted, but the behaviours reveal themselves in stone cold silence, monosyllabic answers and curt, vocal tone.

Get The Audience Involved Early And Often (To Avoid Them Remaining Silent)

One of the most common challenges in a remote environment is the silent audience because it's much easier for a remote group to be literally mute, as opposed to just on mute, than in a face-to-face meeting. Tension increases far more quickly face-to-face because the experience is much more intimate. However, at a distance, the audience is more comfortable to abstain from the discussion and genuinely believe that it's not their responsibility to contribute.

So, when we are leading the remote meeting, our role is to get the audience involved early and often. Being able to do this well requires some preparation. If we've put together a monumentally lengthy deck and only have twenty minutes to deliver it, then the experience is likely to unsatisfactory for all concerned. We must plan the time to ensure there is an opportunity for discussion. If we don't; it's all too easy to fall into the trap of tell, tell, tell. I observed this happen repeatedly throughout my research and whilst it seems so obvious, it's extraordinary how often getting the audience involved early doesn't happen.

So, what practical verbal strategies can we adopt?

- Celebrate success or progress first. We all need some positive news and it's very easy to only ever talk about the negatives. Don't worry; we'll make time to cover the challenges later, after we've warmed people up a bit
- Ask open questions, keep them short and then shut up
- Seek advice and don't set ourselves up as the expert
- Target individuals for a specific question so that they can demonstrate their expertise
- Remind the audience of the meeting objectives and benefits
- Stay open and curious, even when being criticised rather than defensive
- Invite the audience to contribute early and regularly to encourage more awareness and attention to the moments when they might be called upon unexpectedly to contribute.
- Remember, we need to be clear on our process for a remote meeting. By definition, it must be a conversation if we're trying to involve others (rather than a cascade)
- We must always advise the group what we plan to do (e.g. "I will call on you at any point to contribute") because if we don't, then people can feel that this is an aggressive strategy designed to humiliate – which is absolutely not the intention here

Dealing With The Silent Audience

Signposts Matter

As a result of what I have just written, another strategy which is essential in the remote environment is the concept of 'verbal signposts'. A verbal signpost is where we state what we are going to do in the future. A simple example is to say, "I have a question". What follows next? A question of course. Or, "I need to go back to something you said earlier". What follows next? I return to something that was said earlier. The very important point is this: when we let people know what we are going to do, they are not surprised when we subsequently do it. This is *really important* at the start of a call when rapport is low, and using verbal signposts are extremely effective at helping to mitigate the potential for increased tension and actually start warming the group up.

In addition, as part of getting others involved in the discussion, combine a signpost with a name check in order to lessen the sense of being caught out. For example: "I want to ask Bob a question in a moment because I'm really interested in the customer insight data...". Now, if we were Bob, our attention and engagement has just sky-rocketed, because we have been name checked, and we know that a question is coming, so we are alert and waiting for it. Imagine and contrast this approach with: "what should we do about this Bob?" If we were Bob, we didn't know the question was coming and it would be very easy to feel that we are being humiliated, even when this was not the intent. One of the most useful vocal skills to learn in a remote environment is the skill of the verbal signpost. It's extremely effective to reduce tension and increase trust and connection during a remote interaction.

And Don't Forget...

The importance of the visual and non-verbal skills and strategies which I have talked about elsewhere in this book. Starting well means having your camera on, looking at people and not at yoursel), having a neutral expression when listening, smiling from time to time but not too much, slow head nodding in agreement and using your body language effectively to reinforce your message. *All of these things* have a phenomenal impact on our ability to change the mood and connection amongst those in the remote environment. Always show up positively and convey that right from the start; it makes all the difference.

Chapter Eight – Verbal Contributions With Impact

What Underpins Everything

There are some core skills which I coach clients to build when helping them to increase their verbal impact, and I will explore these first in this chapter because they underpin any verbal contribution that we make if we are to sound convincing. We will then explore the power of storytelling as a rich, diverse skill set to learn, before offering a range of other verbal strategies for different scenarios.

Additionally, in terms of those strategies, I have chosen a range of interventions which are critical to master in a remote environment, and again, without apology, I repeat the notion that these will of course work in a face-to-face environment. However, my view is that we can get away with a lot more in we are in the same physical room, because we have other tools in our influencing toolkit to use. Remember, our remote audience might be invisible, which means no cameras turned on, and at times silent (mute on). Therefore, how we deliberately, strategically and effectively leverage the right skill and right strategy in the right way from our verbal toolkit is extremely important in order to have presence remotely.

The Goal Is To Be Visible

Literally and metaphorically. The first rule of conveying presence remotely is by contributing to the conversation in the first place. It's not a win to spend an hour on a call, to say absolutely nothing at all and yet manage to send out a ton of emails. Leadership means visibility. Influence only happens when we are visible to our audience. So, we have to stop lurking in the background. For those of you currently thinking 'but the meeting is a waste of my time!' then my challenge to you is simply this: what have you done to create a more productive use of your time and everyone else's? How are you offering help to create more value? Leadership doesn't happen by invitation. Our role is to shape the discussion in a direction that is more useful. This is a different form of visibility for sure, but a vital one, nevertheless.

Expand Our Linguistic Versatility

All of us have our own unique linguistic style. By this I mean how we characteristically tend to speak using a wide variety of vocal components, including cadence, undulation, use of stories, metaphors, analogies, questions, jokes and the degree to which we are direct or indirect in our approach. Professor Deborah Tannen[27] is a linguistics expert who has extensively researched the words we use, who gets heard and why. She suggests that everything we say functions on two levels. Firstly, language acts as the means by which we communicate information, which is fairly obvious. The second purpose of communication is one that is almost invisible to us, that being the way in which we create rapport with others and how we signal the relative status of individuals within a group.

Many of us have completed over the course of our careers a number of different self-assessments which provide insight into our preferences when it comes to communication. At best we may remember the categorisation. I'm a 'Red' according to Insights[42] for example. The point is that we rarely do more with this information than remember the group to which we belong. However, if we are to have impact at a distance we need to (a) pay attention to how others communicate *differently* to us and (b) flex our own style to be more persuasive. Easy to say for sure, but definitely something which requires deliberate and repeated practice in order to be more influential.

Flex Our Tone Of Voice

Our tone of voice can convert the words in a sentence into a message that sounds like a question, an expression of excitement, an acknowledgement of irritation and many other emotions besides. The point is this: in the absence of the visual, *vocal tone is everything*. We pay more attention to *how* you say it above *what* you say. Positive, or at the very least neutral, is what we are aiming for – especially when our message is contentious. There is a concept called *'the social curiosity phenomenon'*, which essentially says that even if someone was talking about an intrinsically dull topic, they will engage the audience if the speaker sounds enthusiastic about it. This is where variation in vocal tonality comes in. It sounds easy in theory but given that we're all about emotion, and in the moments when we need to disagree the chances are that we will be feeling some emotion, it's much harder to execute than it sounds. We know *exactly* how we sound when we are being sarcastic, confrontational and aggressive.

For women, our natural vocal tonality is at a higher pitch than men and that's a function of biology. A bias that exists for both men and women is that when we hear a high pitch we associate it with immaturity and a lack of authority. One of the reasons why this makes sense is that for all of us, our vocal pitch was much higher when we were children. Women shouldn't try and fake a ridiculous low tone that sounds odd, but what they should do is focus on projecting in the lower part of their range when they need to sound authoritative. This is also easier to do if we all *slow down!*

Slow Down The Pace At Which We Speak

Most people speak far too quickly on conference calls. This also takes practice and muscle memory to *slow down.* Our audience may be international, speaking in their second or third language, and for all of us, battling with the vagaries of creaking internet connections mean that our message will be much less impactful if we are garbling. My recommendation is a half beat slower than our daily conversational speed and if we know that we naturally speak really quickly, then it may require even more of an effort on the brakes. Again, under a degree of pressure or when we are feeling uncomfortable, it's very typical that we speed up, so whilst it's easy to write on a page in a book, it takes repeated and intentional practice so that we can access the skill of speaking more slowly when we need to.

Avoid Rubbish Words

"Do or do not. There is no try". So said Yoda in Star Wars[31]. I've never seen the film but have had this expression quoted back to me repeatedly over the years. I am reminded of it here because it reinforces the power and importance of choosing our words carefully in a remote environment. If we are communicating on a platform where we can't be seen, then our words become our sole tools of influence, so it's vital to understand what does, and does not, have impact. It's also a cause for us to reflect on those unhelpful habits and verbal tics that can impede us, but more on those a little later.

Any word that is overused is a 'rubbish' word. These are the 'verbal crutches' that we use to fill a sentence, when in actual fact it would be better if there were none. 'Sort of', 'kind of like', 'do you know what I mean?' 'Actually', 'you know', 'like' and so on. In fact, any word that is overused in our speech is a 'rubbish' word because it adds no value to what we are saying and sounds like we are uncertain and unconfident. The point is that they are unnecessary in the context of our message and diminish its impact. Our audience becomes distracted, irritated and then fixated on their use, sometimes to the point of counting the 'rubbish' words and ignoring everything else in between. Crisp, clean and concise is the mantra here. Avoiding 'rubbish' words or 'verbal ticks', hesitation and repetition are all key. There is some interesting data that suggests that we are more likely to be persuaded by language that is clear and crisp, rather than when we use lots of 'sentence stuffers' or 'rubbish' words as I call them. We need to simply remove them.

Beware Of 'Management Speak'

What does "*we need to leverage mission critical resources and pivot our mindshare in the right direction*" really mean? Or, how about "*our project recommendations include creating a digital cockpit that will allow us to reach out to stakeholders and socialize content to create consensus in a matrix community*"? What a load of nonsense. I jest not when I say that I have heard both of these phrases in a client environment. Ugh. It has to stop. This is nonsense. The tendency to exaggerate with our language has to be resisted because it doesn't sound clever or convincing. I do appreciate that this is not always easy, not least because organizations, teams, cultures and communities all have words and phrases that make sense *in their world.* Unfortunately, they don't make much sense outside of it. Plus, we want people to remember what we say for the right reasons rather than mock us for the wrong ones.

Beware Of 'Betrayal' Words

There are certain words and phrases that can betray us. What I mean by this is that they can either (a) contradict the intent or the content of our message or (b) reflect that we don't know what to say or (c) reveal a crushing lack of creativity and eloquence. I have spoken elsewhere about the word 'but' and am mindful that some of you will dip in and out of different sections whilst others will read from start to finish. In any event, the purpose is always to cover the content in its wide array of applications, so let me now return to the word 'but'.

There is a colloquial and somewhat crude expression that is 'everything before 'but' is bobbins' (or in actual fact a much stronger word than that). The point is that the use of the word 'but' conveys the message that whatever came before it is either incorrect or untrue. So, if I were to say: "I think you are making a good point but....', it sounds like this isn't really what I think, and it really wasn't a good point. Whilst it might sound as if I am trying to be empathetic and it comes off as disingenuous. I coach my clients to use the word 'and' instead of 'but'.

Another example is the useless phrase 'to be honest with you'. My answer is 'as opposed to what?' Spending the majority of my time lying to you? If we have to label what we're going to say in this way, then it has the unfortunate consequence of indicating that we have been less than straightforward up to now.

At the moment of writing this particular chapter, we all live under the shadow of covid19. Here are some phrases from the UK that I am thoroughly tired of politicians, scientists, politicians and various public figures are repeatedly saying: 'unprecedented times', 'we'll strain every sinew' to overcome this etc. It just sounds tired, unoriginal and after a while, completely disingenuous. We must beware of betraying the impact of our message with this utter nonsense. Whatever our native language, it is filled with a rich diversity of prose which can enhance and engage others. Let's not betray it with a mealy-mouthed selection of trite, tired words and phrases. We will lose our remote audience with their use. There are many different examples; the point with betrayal words is to just remove such language and phrasing from our vocabulary.

Don't Use Weasel Words

There is a subtle difference between weasel words and 'rubbish' words. Reductive words *"just a small point"*, *"quick question"*, *"it's only a little gripe to discuss"* are extremely damaging to the impact of our message. The implication is apologetic, submissive, irrelevant and unfortunately if we think like that, then that's the message we communicate to others. *"I have a point to add"*, or *"I have a question"* or *"there is a gripe we need to discuss"* are what we should be saying – and nothing else. We all have verbal habits and need to be curious about our own bad ones here, and then work to eradicate them.

Instead, Use 'Power' Words

"All words are equal, but some words are more equal than others." So said someone much smarter than I. Essentially, as this chapter has already demonstrated, there are specific words which can make or break a sentence and in addition the examples recently shared, let me add a cross-cultural scenario to the mix. If we were in North America and received feedback on a project that was described as 'quite good', then we should be pleased. This is because 'quite good' means 'really good' and as a phrase it is meant in a complimentary way. However, if we were in the UK and had exactly the same feedback, we would focus on the word 'quite' and it would be interpreted in a derogatory way. In other words, the inference from the word 'quite' would be that our project *wasn't really that great at all.*

Whilst there are vast numbers of books to be written on the topic of cross-cultural communication, this *isn't* one of them. However, the example above does reinforce the importance of the words that we choose to convey impact. Having spent some time talking about what we should not say, now let's turn our attention to words that we could, and should, use.

There has been a wide variety of research completed around the world, whether connected to the psychology of persuasion, the power of words to be used in advertising copy, how we make decisions and even the ways in which we try and attract a partner, all of them focus on the significance of specific words. I call such language 'power words' and have shared a selection that I think are most relevant in the context of communicating remotely. Before jumping in, it is also worth saying that if we overuse these words, then we erode their impact. So, like all good things in life, moderation and intention sit behind these recommendations.

You

Much has been written and published in the copywriting world regarding the power of the word 'you'. There are lists of words that are most likely to grab the attention of the audience and the word 'you' often appears at the top of any such list. The rationale behind this suggests that its power as a word comes from invoking 'the self'. I'm talking about you. This is personal. It matters. Pay attention. When we say 'you' we're publicly attributing something to another person. It's deliberate and therefore you are invested in understanding if what's being said is going to help you, harm you, make you look good, make you look bad, make you feel good, make you feel bad etc. The most significant, personal, powerful thing we can say to another human being is a three-word phrase and one of the words is 'you': 'I love you.' That's the power of the word 'you'.

Our Name

If you read on in this chapter, you will find that this topic is revisited in the context of elegantly interrupting someone. However, for now, let me talk about this as a 'power phrase'. Think about it for a moment. One of the first sounds we learn is the sound of our name. It may not be the first sound we make, but it's certainly one of the first sounds that represents true, deep, significant meaning for us. Our name is intrinsically linked to our identity. When we hear our name, it elicits an instinctive reflex reaction. We tune into others, we check if they are talking to us, about us, inviting us to get involved. I talk more about this in relation to strategies such as 'elegant interruptions' elsewhere in this book, however for now let me say that when we reference people by their name, not only are we making a more direct communication to someone, we are also creating the conditions for social proofing. So, is what you are going to say something that will publicly acknowledge and endorse me, or will it judge and condemn me?

Free

There is some fascinating research which reveals how much we actually love 'free'. Dan Ariely in his book *Predictably Irrational*[33] proved how much we are influenced by the word 'free'. The experiment which he quotes relates to chocolates, and specifically one which pitted Lindt chocolate against Hershey. The trial first invited testers to choose between a chocolate produced by Hershey that only cost one cent. It was a Hershey 'Kiss' versus a chocolate truffle made by Lindt. The Lindt truffle cost fifteen times more, at fifteen cents. The pricing differential for the Lindt chocolate is significant because even at fifteen cents, it was half the normal, expected retail value. Results on first pass suggested that the testers preferred the taste of the Lindt truffle.

However, the second part of the experiment produced different results and the only difference was in the pricing. So, each chocolate experienced the same reduction in price, that being one cent, and this made the Hershey Kiss free. The Lindt chocolate was then worth fourteen cents and so the price difference between chocolates was still the same. There are a number of possible reasons for this, however what Dan Ariely suggests is that 'free' taps into our desire to *not want to miss out.* So, we are certainly incentivised by 'free', plus it represents a no-lose option. In other words, it won't *cost* us anything and so 'we may just as well'. Fascinating isn't it?

Because

Robert Cialdini wrote a fantastic book called *Influence*[14]. In the book, he talks about a world-famous study and as we'll explore momentarily, it stands the test of time despite the fact that the research relates to the heady days of Xerox and their photocopying technology. By the way, when were you last stood at a photocopier? However, I digress. His research focused on how we respond when waiting in line to use the photocopier and faced with the situation where a colleague would like to jump the line, or queue, as we say in the UK. The focus of the research was to understand the response of those who were waiting in line to use the photocopier when someone else, under the guise of being in a hurry, cut in ahead of them to use the photocopier.

During the first round of experiments, the person who was jumping in simply said: "*Excuse me, I have five pages, may I use the Xerox machine?*" When this explanation was given, approximately sixty per cent of those in line allowed the person to cut in ahead of them and use the machine first. In the next scenario, the request was slightly tweaked. This time the person said: "*I have five pages. May I use the Xerox machine, because I'm in a rush?*" There is a small but significant difference between what is said with these two different scenarios. In the second scenario a reason is offered, albeit a very weak one. I mean, who *isn't* in a rush? And frankly, if this research had been conducted in the UK, I cannot help but suggest that such a request would have been given *very short shrift.* However, I digress. To the astonishment of many perhaps, as a result of providing a reason, no matter how flimsy it is, ninety-four per cent of those stood in a line were comfortable to allow the person to push in ahead of them. Astounding it isn't it?

However, Cialdini didn't finish there. In the third and final experiment he instructed the person who was cutting in to make what is an astonishingly facile excuse. This was it: *"Excuse me, I have five pages. May I use the Xerox machine because I have to make copies?"* Quite frankly I find this utterly jaw-dropping. In the UK such a request would be highly likely to elicit some humorous sarcasm at best, or perhaps a mean stare, or at worst, an invitation to go forth and find something better to do with our time. However, no such response was elicited in Cialdini's experiment. Instead, ninety-three per cent still allowed the queue jumper to cut in ahead of them. This is a mere one per cent drop on the previous, flimsy excuse (*"I'm in a rush"*). So, who isn't? This is still an improvement of one third on the first round of experiments.

What was fascinating about Cialdini's research was that he connected it to a fundamental paradigm of human behaviour. In other words, if we provide a reason when we ask others to do a favour for it, then they will be more likely to oblige. It's as simple as that. We need a reason to explain doing what we do. Our audience will want a reason why. Perhaps this is not as daft as it might at first sound. I say this because for those you with children, whether they are small now or not, the first question that they tend to learn very early and repeat very often is the 'why' question. What is also interesting to note is that even if our reason is a weak one, *it is still better than giving no reason at all.*

Means

Our survival mechanism means that the word 'means' means a lot to us. Yes, you read that right. Fundamentally we operate by looking to make association, connection and meaning out of everything that is going on around us. When we are able to make meaning from two different things, then we have more comprehension, comfort and curiosity about what is happening in our world. The rhythm of our daily life means that we are continually learning by processing literally millions of different pieces of sensory information. We find meaning, make connection and as a result, understand more. Oh, and by the way, we will be doing this everyday forever more.

So, what does this have to do with communication and the word 'means' as a power word? Well in essence what it means is that we are already extremely effective at making meanings out of things. According to molecular biologist John Medina from the University of Washington School of Medicine[34], the human brain craves meaning before details. If we don't understand the meaning, then we struggle to absorb the details. So, as an effective communicator, if we can through our message help the audience to make associations, connections and meanings that support the message we wish to create; then we not only are we on to a good thing; but we've earned the right to get into the details.

Instantly

The bottom line is that we want things yesterday. There has been much research completed which would suggest that there are key power words such as 'instant' or 'instantly', 'immediately' or 'right now' that trigger certain parts of our brain into imaging that a reward, treat or something good is coming *very, very soon*. Extensive research into the world of consumer behaviour has shown that in sales, using language such as 'instantly' is extremely effective in driving agreement, action or commitment. All of us have bought products and services online for example, and *absolutely no-one* is persuaded by a message which says: *"please pay for this now, then you can look forward to waiting for days, weeks, months of even years to receive your purchase"*.

New

There is competing and contradictory research in terms of how our brain works when it comes to the word 'new'. There is some consumer data to suggest that consumers prefer established brands and that we like to keep consistency. Don't mess with them seems to be the message on the one hand. However, there is some research that also contradicts this. Part of our brain is stimulated when we are faced with things that are new. In other words, we like the concept of novelty. In terms of communication, what we need to understand is that the word 'new' can trigger a particular response in us; and our challenge is to be clear on what our stakeholders and customers are more likely to be influenced by.

Sorry, But Sorry Is Not A Power Word – Sorry About That

There are a number of words that if we overuse them become an irritant and one such word is 'sorry'. Diet Coke conducted some fascinating research at the beginning of May 2018[21] and suggested that British people apologise on average seven times per day *for absolutely no reason*. Some statistician worked out that this equates to fifty-six hours during the course of a lifetime. In my experience of working with professional men and women over the past fifteen years, there are specific scenarios for which 'sorry' appears to be the means by which to either start, continue or conclude a contribution or message. This is profoundly the wrong tool to use because it damages our brand, reduces our authority and can be extraordinarily annoying. I wonder: do you recognize any of these?

1. *The Conversation Starter:* This is where 'sorry' is used to begin a contribution and it is heard often in a remote environment. For example: "Sorry, can I just say something?" "Sorry, can you just repeat what you've just said?" The word is wrongly used as an attempt to reduce the potential for conflict and not cause offence, because we are asking for another person to give us something: their forgiveness. This automatically puts our interaction on an unequal footing and is to be avoided because it does not convey any confidence or conviction. We should remove it from our language and what we should say instead can be found later in this chapter under the heading of 'Elegant Interruptions'.

2. *The Guilt Maker:* This is where 'sorry' is used in a passive aggressive way to try to encourage the other party to say sorry. So, for example, let's say we are talking, only to then be interrupted by another person. We respond with something like *"sorry, can I just finish my point?"* What is so fascinating about this as a verbal strategy is that (a) we are not sorry at all (b) we are saying sorry when really the other person should because they have done something that might be deemed as rude. The reason why this is called a 'guilt maker' is because it elevates tension in the interaction by trying to shame the other person into realising that they have done something wrong.

3. *The SIB:* This is a three-letter acronym which stands for "Sorry...If...But". So, for example, *"I'm sorry if I caused offence but my point is still valid".* Unfortunately, what this communicates is that we couldn't be *less sorry* if we tried.

The point about the word 'sorry' when communicating remotely is that it is easily and readily used in situations for which it should not. As we've illustrated above! The motive is the desire to not cause offence to the other person; however, there are far more elegant, effective and assertive strategies to use instead and I will talk about them later in this chapter.

Beware The Moving Target

I have been working with a client lately in the media sector. As part of a two-day workshop with senior leaders, we have focused on preparing them for a visit by the Chairman and CEO to the region to review their performance and look ahead at their plans for next year for their businesses. My role was to act as the Chairman and CEO for each of them during a realistic one-hour simulation of the meeting. One leader from the sub-Saharan region reminded me of the concept of 'the moving target' and let me explain how. When I began to scrutinise his performance and the shortcomings for this year, I pushed him to make a commitment for the first half of 2020. His initial reply was "we will definitely make twenty million dollars margin; and the worst case is eighteen million dollars. I am confident we will do twenty million, and probably twenty-one million dollars by the end of May."

Now, let's just reflect on this for a moment. What does it say? Given that the session was taped, it's very easy to highlight a common trap for leaders to watch and listen as they fall into it, that being to move the target under pressure. What his reply had said to me was two things very clearly (1) I'm not confident regarding my commitment (2) I'm already starting to manage expectations regarding it being lower than that which I'm saying I will commit to (3) My commitment to a number doesn't really mean anything. Sounding authoritative, sounding credible and sounding like there is conviction in what we say is something we all want to communicate. However, there are many different ways in which we can achieve the exact opposite, and this is one of them. Getting it right, being clear and being consistent is essential. Face-to-face this is hard enough, but remember, in a remote environment we have got very little information to work with and will jump on top of this language immediately.

The Power Of Hyperbole

Hyperbole is exaggeration. It's the opposite of understatement and originates from a Greek word meaning 'over-casting'. What is its purpose? The intent of such language is emphasis and memorability. Our language is littered with hyperbole and it can be an extremely effective approach to making our point. There are millions of examples of hyperbole – starting with what I have just written. Hyperbole is not *literally true*. What is true however is that there are examples of hyperbole that include "I'm so hungry I could eat a horse", or "I died of embarrassment', or "she's as old as the hills" etc. So, why is it such a fascinating and effective approach to communication – especially when communicating remotely? Many different reasons including using hyperbole within our commentary can re-engage the audience and make them sit up and pay attention.

Throughout history are examples of hyperbole in public speeches that have stood the test of time, and one of the most famous came from President John F Kennedy who was describing Thomas Jefferson at a White House state dinner to honour forty-nine Nobel prize winners. What Kennedy said was: "I think this is the most extraordinary collection of human talent, of human knowledge, that has ever been gathered at the White House, with the possible exception of when Thomas Jefferson dined alone."

Another example from US folklore and the character Paul Bunyan, who looms large as a giant lumberjack. An opening line attributed to 'Babe the Blue Ox' is one where winter is described as follows: "well now, one winter it was so cold that all the geese flew backward, and all the fish moved south and even the snow turned blue. Late at night, it got so frigid that all spoken words froze solid afore they could be heard. People had to wait until sunup to find out what folks were talking about the night before."

Isn't that fantastic? It's prose which makes us sit and pay attention and effectively that's exactly what we're trying to do. I have written repeatedly in this book that in a remote environment we might not be able to see or hear from our audience. Quite frankly, we don't know if they're unloading the dishwasher rather than listening fully to us. We're constantly striving to reach people remotely and what hyperbole does do is accentuate our language in a way that can make our point land and be remembered. Use it well, use it intentionally and notice what happens.

Perfect Pronouns

Writing this book has presented all sorts of interesting challenges and one of the biggest is the use of pronouns. Do I use 'we'? Do I use 'I'? Do I use 'you'? In the context of disagreeing without being disagreeable, about which I spoke earlier, what is true is that the pronoun 'you' has the potential to be incendiary. Why? Because it's personal. When was the last time you felt good as a result of being told that *you* were wrong? It can sound like an attack and I coach clients to use it with care. As a contrast, a very powerful use of the 'you' pronoun is when someone warrants appreciation, acknowledgement, positive feedback because of the quality of their work or contribution.

Equally, we have to be careful of the use of the word 'we'. It can create tension when what we need to use is 'I' or 'you'. See? It's a minefield. Our challenge when making effective verbal contributions is to ensure that we use *exactly the most appropriate* pronoun for our message, in order to continuing to engage and persuade the audience. If we do not, it the pronoun that creates the problem.

Stories: The Basis Of Any Great Persuasive Contribution

I talk about stories in several different parts of this book deliberately and repeatedly because of the nature of how I wrote it and designed it to be used. You may, dear reader, dip in and out of different sections and so not see where I wrote about it elsewhere. It has so many different, entirely relevant and extremely effective applications, so I make no apology for revisiting it. Becoming a masterful storyteller, and by which I mean someone who can convey crisp, concise and compelling messages to influence others, is the absolutely *most powerful influencing skill that we can learn.*

Given that we are talking about interventions with impact in this chapter, whether it be to answer a question, deal with a challenge, handle resistance, explain something complicated, ask for help, increase urgency around an issue, create excitement, increase engagement, handle an objection *or for any other reason where we need to influence others,* the skill we need to master is the skill of telling stories.

Much has been written in the world of leadership development about the power of storytelling and we know it's a topic about which I can wax lyrical. For the purposes of our conversation here, I want to be clear on the definition. Again, and to repeat, a story is simply a message that is structured to inspire and influence our audience.

A story is not the same as an anecdote. For example: "let me tell you about the time when I fell out of a helicopter....". A story as I describe it is when those moments in the conversation arrive where we need to *change the other person.* We need to change their perspective, change their mind, change their course of action, change their level of enthusiasm, change their level of commitment and so on. And either we are successful, or we are not. It is the moments when through our verbal contribution we engage, we influence, and we persuade others. The technology that has been built to do this brilliantly and consistently is the technology of stories. They have been around for millennia, long before computers and long before paper were invented. They are what have enabled tribes, countries, faiths, religions, cultures, rituals, families and communities to stay together and thrive together. So, we would do well to learn from what works.

There are a number of components which transform our verbal messaging into a powerful and persuasive story, and the most critical are explored in more detail over the next few pages.

The Hook

Any great story grabs our attention. Think about a James Bond movie[32] for a moment. It is the only franchise where, instead of endless, tedious credits at the beginning of the movie, there is an action sequence designed to lure the audience in, heighten their sense of anticipation and engagement with what will happen next. It's designed to create a sense of literally being on the edge of our seats. The sequence ends with a crescendo and then cue the new James Bond theme tune. As the audience we are excited, satisfied and looking forward to what comes next.

In the world of business, a 'hook' or 'attention grabber' requires subtlety and context and there are many different ways to do it (see below!) Using humour or being playful *can work* and as always, it requires reading the room effectively and being skillful. Our knowledge of the audience on the call and our level of relationship with them will affect the risk behind this strategy. Alternatively, using a quote or a saying that is relevant provides a great way to convey impact. It shouldn't be excessive or uncomfortably theatrical either, it's just about being distinguishable and able to have that 'stand out' capability.

The evidence for the effectiveness of such a strategy comes from Claus Moller[15]. Claus Moller[15] is a leadership consultant who has spent more than half a century focused on leadership development and has achieved some extraordinary success in supporting global industries around the world. Of the many things about which he writes, one of his pieces of research really caught my attention. Moller found that we have between four and fourteen words in which to achieve a 'moment of truth' with the person to whom we are speaking. A 'moment of truth' is a simply a decision point and the context from Moller's perspective is a decision point regarding whether to build or strengthen our rapport with another person – or not. In other words, four to fourteen words are the basis on which to decide if this is someone with whom my connection is going to grow, or if it is going to wane. Now of course, this is not a conscious decision, but we all make them. This is also not meant to suggest that 'the die is cast' after just fourteen words. It is not. We can make a mess of things and rectify it later, but the relevance of this insight when it comes to remote communication is important.

Think about it for a moment. Another person on the call starts to speak and we all know that we make a decision, fast, about whether or not they are worth listening to anymore. If it is positive, then we lean in, pay closer attention and are engaged. If the decision goes against the speaker, then we metaphorically sit back, reduce our attention and at worst, are already hitting the mute button and turn our attention to other things.

I talk about the 'hook' in communication. What I mean by this is a phenomenon that I have witnessed many times over the years in sales calls, pitches and meetings and it is why the Moller[15] research makes such sense. Just recently, I have been working with General Managers of a global healthcare business where their role is to win, and retain, the attention of their line manager. The organisation is fast paced, flat (so a matrix structure), full of remote teams, highly entrepreneurial, driving change, reducing complexity and focused on fostering a bolder culture where they 'fail fast' and move forward to drive value for their customers, plus growth and profitability for the business. These are senior leaders and be under no illusion that these skills are easy. I have been working with them to make their messages more crisp, concise and compelling. We have combined theory with repeated skills practice and believe me; it's a work in progress.

I believe that we have between six to ten seconds at most to hook our audience, convey presence and demonstrate impact through our contribution. We have this small window during which we need to entice, attract, intrigue, compel, appease, enthuse and motivate the listener to do just that: keep listening. If we don't, we are lost to others who become increasingly frustrated with our failure to make any kind of sense. Our presence and ability to influence evaporates and the message we wanted to communicate is sunk. I remain astonished at the number of people who simply don't get it. "But my message is so important!" "I've got great information", "No-one ever listens to what I say" are the cries I often hear. The fact is that if we haven't got the hook right, then no one cares about our great information because they have already stopped listening.

So, what we need is for our opening gambit to hook the audience in. There are so many examples of a hook and it will vary dependent on whether we are responding to a contribution of another person, or whether we are trying to lead the conversation by stating a message, or beginning a pitch, of our own. However, some examples of hooks with which I have been working of late include the following:

(a) Speak To My Priorities

Everyone in business is measured in some way or another, and this is, first and foremost, what we all care about. Why? Because it's business and how on earth are we going to be able to justify that we have done a great job at the end of the year? Never mind seek that pay rise or performance related bonus. In order to be persuasive to others in business we need to know what they care about. What are they being measured on delivering to the business? What are they under pressure to achieve? What scrutiny will they face if expectations are not met? Our story, our message, our perspective has to be framed within their context, otherwise we are assuming that others can join the dots themselves. They haven't got time; won't do it and we do not ultimately get what we want from the interaction. Now, everything I have just written is true for a face-to-face conversation as well. However, in a remote environment where we are struggling to get, and then keep, the audience's attention, a sure-fire way to enable this is to talk about the audience's KPIs. Trust me; even if they had been cranking out emails, walking the dog and making a coffee, they will pay attention now.

For example, if we are pitching to a sales leader who is focused on increasing profit from the existing client base, a simple example of a hook might be: "*I have an idea that will help drive profit from one of our biggest clients*". Or, "*We have a great example to share of how we increased margin by 20% on our last deal".* We get the point. Speak to what is uppermost in my mind, my key performance indicators (KPIs), goals, objectives or whatever we wish to call it and I will be (at least in the short term), hooked.

(b) Appeal To My Communication Style

If we are effective at 'reading the room' or 'reading people', then our hook can be one that appeals to the emotional state or preference of the other person. If we know that the other person likes analogy, metaphor, colloquialism, a soundbite etc. then we should start with one ourselves. Remember, it can't be too long. If, on the other hand, we are talking to a data, facts, figures person then clearly the strategy has to be the opposite. Provide me with a memorable fact, give me a statistic I will like or offer a piece of data that will stand out. We'll pay attention. Our challenge is to be flexible with our approach.

(c) Be Contentious

This isn't as aggressive or argumentative as it sounds. In other words, the purpose of the hook here is to create attention through challenge. I hear a lot in business today of the need for leaders to be more disruptive. The intent behind this wish is to shake things up, challenge convention, think outside of the norms. When we publicly dissent or question a viewpoint, we are in effect, questioning those in the audience who hold that opinion. The notion of social proofing, so validating each other through public recognition, is scrutinised. Our contribution doesn't have to be theatrical; a simple statement such as 'I disagree' is an assertive but not aggressive way to gain the attention of others, not least because they want to understand why.

(d) Make Me The Hero

If our hook is about making me look like the 'good guy' then rest assured, you will have my attention. It goes without saying that our approach needs to be both authentic as well as relevant to discussion at hand. However, a hook that is based around public recognition of a colleague for their contribution, success, track record, question or challenge, will guarantee that particular individual's attention.

(e) Start With The Key Question

One of the ways to get the attention of the virtual room is to start with a critical question that is overarching any specific discussion. So, for example, I have had a recent scenario at the time of writing this book that involved one of my global car manufacturing clients. They were discussing a customer experience that was far from satisfactory. This particular customer had been loyal to the brand for the past ten years and had recently part exchanged their vehicle for an almost new model. As someone who had been loyal to the brand for the last 10 years, this is the type of individual that manufacturers want to engage with in order to drive loyalty and advocacy. From my client's perspective, and as can all too often happen, the discussion degenerated into a 'who is going to pay to fix this?' issue between the sales and aftersales departments. As the blame and counter blame game moved backwards and forwards between the leaders of these teams, it was the Managing Director began his contribution with a great hook in the form of a question. He said: "how much will this cost us if we *don't* do the right thing?" As a hook, this suspended the financial tussle underway between his leaders, and instead focused the conversation on the most important component: the customer. His supplementary comments were powerfully in support of getting past the issue of payment and focused on the issue of speed to resolution.

(f) Engage With A Sound-Bite

According the Cambridge Dictionary[17], the definition of a soundbite is 'a short sentence or phrase that is easy to remember.' Unfortunately, it continues 'these are often included in a speech made by a politician and repeated in newspapers and on television and radio.' The reason that I say 'unfortunately' is because there is a brand association with politicians and soundbites that is usually not positive. Their soundbites can be associated with being vacuous, overly simplistic, insincere, evasive, superficial and pointless. Clearly, we are not trying to achieve any of this with a soundbite. Rather, its purpose is to create simplicity from complexity, make memorable something that is easy to forget, and it most certainly *does need* to be relevant, sincere, helpful and memorable. For example, one of my clients from the world of telecommunications used 'perfect gets in the way of good'. His point was to drive greater impetus, agility and action across his organisation and was frustrated with what he viewed as an unhelpful desire to want to make everything 'just so' before going to market. It's a great soundbite. Often metaphor and analogy can also help here. A recent example with a client related to a complex manufacturing process and an embedded supplier. The client was looking to a short-term gain through changing some aspects of the process and by changing quality components around the finished product. Given that over four thousand parts are involved, there is a level of detail and complexity behind the reasons why taking such an approach is a really bad commercial idea. "This is like throwing grass seeds on concrete". The intent behind the metaphor is convey the message that what was being recommended wouldn't work - ever.

(g) Show That You Get My World

This is subtly different to speaking to my priorities and is more about using my language, lexicon and terminology. All industries and organisations have certain words, phrases, soundbites and acronyms that are peculiar to their 'world', and by matching them with our choice of language what we demonstrate is that we are part of their crew, we are like them, we are one of them. To be clear, it is *essential* that we really do understand what we are saying, because bluffing it is a guarantee of being found out, and hence our credibility is destroyed – permanently. Social tension is highest at the start of an interaction, and this is a great way to reduce that tension and increase rapport.

(h) Show That You've Done Your Homework

This strategy is fundamentally about demonstrating credibility by sharing a concise piece of data. For example, this could be about the company, the competition, the market etc. that will not be readily known to others. Personally, customer insights are always extremely powerful because quite simply our customers determine our success and we can't argue with our customers!

If I am responding to a contribution made by someone else, examples of hooks can include:

- Agreeing with them as we then move into our point
- Providing a 'verbal stroke' (no this isn't filthy; it's an appreciation of what they have said in a genuine, authentic way)
- A soundbite (in other words a short expression or saying, often metaphorical, with a cadence and imagery that is very powerful)

- A short commentary which has its own, three-part narrative structure

Always Have A Narrative Structure

The most effective stories are split into three parts: a beginning, middle and end. The brilliant thing about a narrative structure is that it enables logic, sequence and flow to the message and without it, we can just waffle for hours. A narrative structure is where there are three chapter headings or section titles to the message. Examples of a narrative structure could include:

- This Is What It Is, This Is What It Does, This Is Why It Matters
- Problem, Opportunity, Action
- Wins, Learns, Next Steps
- What Worked, What Didn't, What We Must Do Now

The list is endless. We can create our own narrative structures. The point is that as a structured message for impact, we *must have them and must say them*, in order to help our audience to understand where we are in our story, and to help make our point resonate.

Get The Amount Of Detail Right

Most people talk too much and say too little. The amount of detail we should include is determined by two things (a) our goal for the message or story and (b) the narrative structure. All too often in the absence of clarity on one or both of these things, then we can talk, and talk, and talk. I call it 'blah, blah, blah' or 'weapons grade waffle'. I have been working with high potential talent in the life sciences profession recently who need to pitch ideas to senior leaders to garner support to take their recommendations into the business. One of the *most common* mistakes is too much detail. It comes from a place of having a need to 'prove' ourselves I think. Or perhaps it is a habit that kicks in when we are under pressure. With the lack of narrative structure and goal clarity for the message, time and again what I observe is long, granular, overly detailed answers and this must be avoided. Say less; influence more. That's a motto to live by in the remote environment *for certain*.

If It's Good, It's Got A STAR Moment

STAR is an acronym. Quite simply it stands for 'something they'll always remember'. Think for a moment about somebody in your life who is funny or fascinating. They will be a natural storyteller and as part of their skill set, what exists within their stories are STAR moments. These are the moments that connect us totally, meaningfully and memorably to what is being said. Great stories are remembered and repeated. That means they also have at least one STAR moment. These moments can be a number, a phrase, a saying, a metaphor or analogy, a quote, a fact within our message that STAND OUT. If it's effective, STAR moments make our story memorable and repeatable.

Metaphor and Analogy Can Help

We are wired for metaphor and analogy and all of us, irrespective of our culture or background, have been brought up on an extraordinary array of phrases and expressions that brilliantly express a fundamental truth. A complicated, complex message can be massively helped by the use of a metaphor or analogy. I remember my first boss said to me "you don't have a dog and bark yourself". After all this time, I still remember it, use it and it's a great illustration of a point about utilising the right resources for the job. A note of caution is advised for an international audience, that being that some metaphors and analogies don't literally translate. For example, the analogy of 'I know them like the back of my hand' makes sense to a native English speaker, however if it was said to an Italian, then it would make no sense at all. Their equivalent expression would be 'I know them like I know my chickens'.

Be Clear On The 'Ask'

Whether we're pitching an idea, responding to a question, dealing with a pushback or responding to another perspective, we should know what we want and be clear on asking for it. Do we want a decision, an action or a commitment? Beware of this one because in the absence of a clear ask, guess what most teams default to? *More discussion.* When in doubt, 'let's keep talking about it' is the all too often repeated mantra at the end of sub-optimal meetings. On some occasions this is the correct next step; on most occasions it is not. As a result, businesses and teams are less agile than they could be. Beware.

The Iterative Ask

Imagine a pond that we have to get across. We cannot cover the pond in one leap, we need stepping stones to get to the other side. This is a metaphor for an 'iterative ask'. An iterative ask is simply to achieve agreement to something big; we get there by securing commitment to a number of smaller things in sequence. When trying to drive change, we must beware of asking for something that is too large, too overwhelming, too difficult to comprehend for a team, an organisation or board to agree to all at once. What is far more effective, and far more influential, is when we are able to ask for a small commitment. Once secured, we need to show success, make the person or team who agreed to it look like a hero, and then go back and ask for more. We have a much greater chance of being successful in the long term versus putting all our hopes on a big ask. Remember that in a challenging economy, turbulent economic times, fast pace and high risk the easiest thing to do *is nothing at all*. That's why the big ask is even more challenging to get over the line. I'm not saying it's not possible; it is with strategy, skill and persistence. What I am saying is that the iterative ask is a very powerful approach to use as an alternative.

Sign Off On A High

In the 1970s and 1980s in the UK, there was a famous comedy duo who had their own TV programme called 'The Two Ronnies'[30]. A family favourite, this hour-long show ran on British television with two gentlemen, both named 'Ronnie' funnily enough, and it contained an amusing variety of skits, monologues, songs, jokes and sketches. As a duo, they were renowned at the end of every show for signing off with one Ronnie saying: *'and it's goodnight from me'* with the other Ronnie replying with *'and it's goodnight from him'*.

By now you may be wondering....so what has that got to do with me? Well, in the world of leadership communication, the short answer is 'a lot'.

As an example, one of my clients is a life sciences business with whom I worked to help some of their technical leaders become more effective in their ability to influence their colleagues across the organisation. Whilst professionals are often taught to hone their pitch, rehearse their opening line and handle the tricky question, we have spent a considerable amount of time talking about the 'sign-off'. Quite simply the sign-off is the end of our message. It is our parting shot, our last impression, our verbal full stop.

In my experience, the sign-off is often extremely weak. If it is in response to a question, if it is answering a criticism, if it is pitching an idea or if it is something else, the conclusion of our verbal intervention can easily be very weak. Whether it is the relief of getting to the end of what we wanted to say, or the prospect of not having to face the audience for much longer, all too often there is a lame 'thank you' or 'that's it'. Candidly, if we need to say: 'that's it', then our message isn't sufficiently structured and obvious to our audience, and it should be.

Quite simply we need to stop this. Remember that we have just been talking about the concept of an ask. So, wherever possible, we should look to ensure our contribution ends with a connection back to the ask that we have, or the point that we have made. Our tempo, tonality and energy should also be similar at the end to the way in which we started. Otherwise we are in danger of sounding like we are running out of energy ourselves for the idea.

The Handoff

There are instances where we do not have an ask per se and might just be that we are responding to a contribution from someone else. In which case we still need to finish our contribution on a high by signalling to the audience several things (a) we have finished (b) we have completed a compelling point (c) it is now the turn of the listener to speak. The possibilities are endless for what we can do, but it needs to be natural, impactful and an easy invitation to move the conversation forward. In a face-to-face environment, the fact that we can see and sense the reaction of the people in the room, and we can both deploy non-verbal gestures and signals to indicate to someone that we want them to speak, all makes it potentially easier to get a response. However, let's consider for a moment what happens in a remote environment.

I was on a remote call only recently where the point was perfectly demonstrated on a number of occasions. A leader in a manufacturing business was explaining the rationale for a new process to a sales audience. He did so, and then asked the (fatal) question: "what do you think?" Guess what the response was? Stone, cold silence. Whilst this becomes uncomfortable if it persists, the audience has been given permission to not take responsibility for answering; hence the awkward silence. The other piece about this open question is simply that it might not be the right question to ask at all. My view is that we need to be really thoughtful and planned about what we really want as a response from the audience when we hand off control of the conversation to them. Remember it should always link back to our goal.

For example: 'Anthony, what do you think?' makes sense if our goal is to get Anthony's commitment to our recommendation. *'David, how can we do this?'* would make sense if our goal is to get David and his team to take action. 'I'm wondering Jackie how much you would be willing to contribute from your Q2 budget...?' would work if our goal is to get Jackie to put her hand in her pocket and pay for something. All of these will work well. Remember, if we have a specific ask, we can link our point back to the ask (e.g. for a decision, action of some type of commitment).

It is also important to reiterate the importance of our style in how we convey the message. I am not a fan of pitching in the traditional sense of the word. It's slightly too forceful, slightly too polished, slightly too turbo charged. We are talking about being natural, relaxed, articulate and composed in our delivery and in the way that we finish our message.

Reading The Room

This is the ability to understand the mood, energy, response, emotion in the room. It is a fast-changing dynamic and a continual need, rather than a one-off activity. It's the skill of observing the visual, verbal and non-verbal cues, be they large and small, plus silence, and correctly choosing the response we should make to it. Clearly this is much easier to do if we are in the same room face-to-face because remotely, our audience might be invisible and for large proportions of the time, mute. This means that all kinds of micro gestures on which we would normally rely have been removed. So, what can we do? As I have mentioned elsewhere, model the behaviour that we want others to demonstrate by turning our camera on and asking others to do the same. And if they do not? Or if it's not that easy for people to turn their cameras on? There are a range of strategies that get the audience involved and encourage them to increase their engagement with and contribution to the conversation. Let's explore the most effective ones now.

Verbal Strategies That Add Value In A Group

Peter Honey and Neil Rackham conducted some powerful research that explored the most effective verbal strategies to drive understanding in a group. Having worked extensively with clients in both a face-to-face and remote environment, these strategies are incredibly useful when looking to convey impact remotely. For example:

Making Suggestions (Content or Procedure): This is very self-explanatory and involves proposing either a particular topic to discuss or, advising the order of topics to be discussed. So, an example we could say: "Bob, let's talk about the budget now". This is a suggestion for content. Or we could say: "Bob, let's talk about headcount and then go back to budget and customer queries later". This is a suggestion for procedure.

Building: The notion here is simply adding to an existing idea. For example, if someone suggested that we meet at 10am on Thursday on a remote platform, a way of building on that idea would be to say: "yes let's do that and I'll send the data we need to discuss out to everyone by Tuesday night so that they can review it in advance."

Supporting: This is simply agreeing with the contribution of another person. So, we might say "I agree with Bob" or "Natasha has made a great point". Demonstrating support is a great way to invest in the emotional bank account of others.

Bringing In: This strategy is about encouraging the contributions of others. So, for example, we might say "I would be interested to hear from Lorna". "We haven't heard from Mandy so far, and I so wonder, what her views are?" The point about this strategy is that it needs to sound encouraging and inclusive. It cannot sound like we're trying to catch out a colleague who we think has become distracted and is currently loading the dishwasher.

Shutting Out: This is not as aggressive as it might sound. I have just spoken about the scenario where we need to encourage *more contribution*. Let's imagine for a moment where we have an individual on the call where what we need to do is encourage *less* contribution. Again, we do not want to turn this person into a hostile attendee, and we need to maintain a positive balance in relation to their emotional bank account. *How* we say it, is as important as *what* we say. For example, using clear, neutral tone what we could say is: "Jane, I'm very grateful to you for your comments so far and I'm curious to understand what John thinks about this?" The point is that we've shown appreciation for Jane (this is a deposit in their emotional bank account), whilst asking her to stop talking (this is a withdrawal from her emotional bank account). This latter example is a way in which we can challenge and orchestrate the contributions being made, without causing damage to the relationship that we have.

Testing Understanding: It does precisely what it says on the tin. This is a strategy that allows for a pause in the progression of the conversation and an evaluation of whether or not everyone is still on the same page. For example: "let me see if I've understood you correctly. Did you just say...?" The reason why this is so helpful is because in a fast paced, attention deficit environment we can forget to do this. One of Stephen Covey's habits from *Seven Habits Of Highly Effective People* explores the notion of seeking first to understand, before being understood.

Summarising: We don't have to be the formal chair of the call, or the host of it. Anyone can do this, and we should if and when our sense is that we need to. For example: "we've agreed to do x, y, z." The value of this particular approach is in stopping endless reiteration of the same point by multiple people on a call. This is an extraordinarily common and infuriating practice. We do not have to be the most senior person or the owner of the meeting to step in do this. One of my expressions is that 'leadership doesn't happen by invitation". It happens by those who choose to show initiative and demonstrate it.

Question To Understand Reasons: "Why do you want to do that?" "Why is that important to you?" Tonality is important here to avoid this sounding aggressive. It is a classic 'seek first to understand before being understood' strategy and can avoid much subsequent and unnecessary tension. A side note on questions please. Too many leaders ask dreadful questions. They are too long, too complex, stacked with multiple questions all posed simultaneously and then combined with opinion. These are very poor skills and we must stop it. Ask short, clear questions and never underestimate the power of shutting up.

Question To Understand Feelings: "What's behind this emotion?" Why are you unhappy?" There is a slight health warning around my second example for a couple of reasons. The first is that whenever we ask the question 'why', it will naturally elicit an answer beginning with 'because'. 'Because' is a word that encourages us to move into a more defensive place. As a result, maintaining a neutral and curious tone is important.

Being Open: This strategy requires high levels of emotional intelligence and management of self because it means *describing* our emotions rather than *displaying* our emotions. For example, "I'm really unhappy at the direction of this conversation". Or alternatively "I am very frustrated by the decision to move this project in a different direction." Easy to say; much harder to do.

Defending/Attacking: Honey and Rackham described this strategy as such, and I'm not a fan of 'attacking' because the guarantee is a fight, with massive amounts of withdrawals from each other's emotional bank accounts and all for what? I believe in being strong and pushing back; but doing so around the issue rather than the person. Defending our position is perfectly reasonable, but removing emotion, remaining calm and being crisp and concise in our defence is key. Equally, an 'attack strategy' doesn't need to be aggressive. Considered, calm challenge and scrutiny is the order of the day here.

Giving Information: A basic verbal strategy but all too often it goes wrong. Too much information, a lack of narrative structure, irrelevant and trivial data and no logical conclusion to our contribution are just some of the errors made with this approach. We've all been in meetings and on calls where someone is just going on....and on....and on.

Interrupting: This is demonstrated by cutting across a conversation to such an extent that the flow of information stops. I have spoken earlier in the chapter about how to do this elegantly.

Disagreeing: In addition, I have spoken elsewhere about the strategy of doing this in a way that doesn't damage the relationship. I call it 'disagreeing without being disagreeable'. Take a look and practise it. If we want to be influential, we need to be really good at doing this. The easy way out is to say nothing and then comment later. That's not influence; that's a lack of confidence and leadership. Sometimes we want to be very direct. Simply say 'I disagree'. I'm not being facetious! Don't sugar coat it; don't explain at length; don't ask for forgiveness. Just say it and then move on.

Answering Questions In General

Our first challenge as leaders is to connect questions to engagement. It means our audience are listening, which is a huge win, rather than cranking out those emails once more. Our second challenge is to become comfortable with and embrace the reality that we should expect to be scrutinised. Our third and final challenge is to become effective at answering these questions. Some first principles: slow down, take our time, listen, think, and then answer. These incredibly simple and effective strategies are often roundly ignored in a remote environment. Perhaps this is because we might not be able to see the other party, or perhaps it is because we immediately feel threatened or attacked due to a lower level of trust in a remote environment. Whatever the reason, our opportunity here is to convey presence by taking a moment to gather our thoughts *before tackling the question.* All too often there is a rush to respond, justify a position, over explain a process and generally complicate and confuse the listener. In addition:

- Never attempt to answer a question which isn't clear. Ask the questioner to clarify.
- If we are asked multiple questions at once, again, don't attempt to answer them all; seek more clarity first.
- Avoid lengthy answers – they suggest a lack of confidence in our message. Less is always more.
- Don't 'seek approval' for the answer – just move on!

Answering Questions In Particular

Our audience can be challenging in a variety of different ways. If the question is irrelevant, then answer briefly and politely. A swathe of sarcasm or condescension is never appreciated. If we are interrupted, we have choices. We can (a) answer the question and carry on (b) answer and ask for further questions to be held to the end if we are pitching or using slides (c) advise that we will answer the question in a few moments. If we are faced with argumentative behavior, then we really do need to carry on reading, because the 'reframe' technique is extremely effective.

The Reframe

This is a very powerful tool to use to handle challenge from the audience, particularly when what we are hearing might be deemed as overtly critical, or even something more personal, or even hostile. There are lots of practical uses of this tool as it comes from the world of Neuro Linguistic Programming (NLP), and I use it with my clients in this specific context. In other words, whilst the temptation might be to respond in kind when someone says something negative or even rude, aggressive or pointed, we will always convey more presence if we are able to channel a potentially emotive and challenging moment into a more positive and engaging direction for the discussion.

So, let's take a real example which I have observed as part of my research for this book. Imagine for a moment that someone expresses some frustration with us, or a member of our team. Let's imagine that they say, "your team aren't able to effectively deal with the calls from our customers when they ring the call centre". Now, imagine if we were the leader running the call centre team. Naturally our tendency would be to leap to the defence of those who work for us and/or attack the individual who said what they did. The reframe technique enables us to avoid that possibility and instead, take control of the conversation in a positive and productive direction. I coach my clients to do 4 things:

1. **Keep Listening!** Believe me, it's very easy to stop listening when we think we're being attacked.
2. **Be Curious To Understand The Underlying Motive**. We won't know what this is if we are not listening properly. So, in this example, it might be action or customer service. In other words, the other party is really interested in getting things done, or engaging customers, or ensuring that customers are not disappointed in our service. The point is, they are not really interested in causing maximum harm and offence.
3. **Change The Focus Of The Question To Find Common Ground**. Again, in this example we might say "what's important to both of us is providing the best customer service". Or, we might say "so what I've heard is that getting the project closed by Friday is very important to you. The way in which we can achieve that is....." The point is that we are demonstrating that (a) we have

heard and (b) we have understood the point of the other person. This is so critical because *not being listened to* is one of the most frustrating things that we can do to others.

4. **Take The Heat Out Of It.** This means not reacting to the emotion being communicated. Convert the judgement or aggression into a neutral statement, and then add our own perspective to it. Certainly, it is always easier said than done, but essential to avoid the tempo and tension increasing in the conversation. Practical ways to improve through practice include (a) asking for challenge in a safer environment e.g. practising with our team or line manager to meaningfully build skill (b) join a debating group or speakers' association. They are fantastic in providing multiple opportunities to develop this skill every week in most countries around the globe.

The Clean Answer (Avoid Too Much Information - TMI)

There are many things that I love about my work, one of which is the opportunity to observe my clients in action, in order to provide rich and extensive feedback on their strengths, as well as those areas for growth. One such occasion really struck me of late and, with my client's permission because he reads my newsletter, he has allowed me to share. Recently, I had the opportunity to observe a senior sales leader conduct a sales meeting. He had all his functional and regional leaders in the room and during the course of the three-hour meeting he was asked a question by one of his team members. So far, there is nothing at all unusual with this situation. However, his answer *was fascinating* because it lasted for five minutes. *Yes, five minutes straight.* At times the content was witty, amusing and insightful. However, for the vast majority of the time the content was mired in detail, irrelevant and frustrating to the listener. It was also just *far too long*. The acronym TMI (Too Much Information) was in full force with this explanation.

The experience got me thinking..........what's really going on here? The question posed was very clear and simple, the answer given most certainly was not. He was seduced into a mammoth amount of over-explaining. We live in an attention deficit business environment where most people aren't listening most of the time and when I debriefed with the client, he was gracious enough to acknowledge a number of things:

1. He didn't really hear the question properly.
2. He believes that he needs to prove he knows a lot of things to his colleagues.
3. He enjoys 'taking the floor' to share his point of view.

Now, before any of us leaps to judgement, *as human beings* we all seek different forms of validation from our communication with others. Whilst our motivations might be similar or different to those of my client, the reality is that what we believe impacts how we communicate and at times, this can work against us. In this instance, it was preventing my client from being crisp, concise and compelling with his communication.

As a result, we have been working on what I term 'the clean answer'. In other words, think of what you hear when you listen to a politician being interviewed by the media and recognise that I am talking about *the complete opposite of that.* Whilst I appreciate that this is a generalisation, all too often what I hear are long, irrelevant, pre-scripted answers that are not connected to the question posed, and when politicians do this, they actually create more difficulty for themselves by providing more material for the reporter to scrutinise.

The clean answer technique is all about answering the question asked, resisting the temptation to provide all the backstory, avoiding the trap of being defensive in offering rationales for things that were never sought in the question, stepping away from all the detail and, knowing when to quickly ***stop talking.*** This is an incredibly powerful communication technique and one that works well face to face, is extremely effectively in the remote meeting environment *and absolutely essential* when pitching to senior leaders.

I have a client who puts their top talent through a fantastic development opportunity that includes intensive skills development, 1:1 coaching, involvement in critical strategic projects, and a chance to pitch out ideas to the executive team at the end of a nine to twelve-month period. My role has been to coach the delegates to create and communicate a compelling story and handle executive level scrutiny. One fantastic leader with whom I have worked learned this lesson brilliantly. She began her journey with endless explanation, but finished it with near monosyllabic answers when questioned intensively during her pitch. As a result, the confidence she conveyed was fantastic, the message was persuasive, and the audience were convinced. Say less and convey more impact. Answer the question and nothing else. Be brief, be brilliant and be done.

Stick To The Rule Of No Nasty Surprises

One of the topics about which I speak is the challenge of pitching to a democracy. This about how to be influential with teams of stakeholders and one of the components of doing this well is the rule of 'no nasty surprises'. In essence, there are times when we have to convey bad news or say something that others do not want to hear. I am *not suggesting that we sugar coat it*. What I am suggesting is that we need to be strategic and collaborative in the way that we prepare our audience to hear the message. A simple example might be one used with one of my clients recently. They are a brand manager for a fashion brand where one of the product lines has delivered disappointing sales. Whilst the downward direction of the sales line cannot be denied, to simply present it to a wider leadership group without preparing the sales leader ahead of time would have been an enormous mistake. The sales leader needed to know and understand the context in which these results would be shared. They also needed the opportunity to prepare their story in response to the guaranteed scrutiny under which the rest of the organisation would undoubtedly put them. Remember, leadership is a relationship business. If we throw someone under the bus in this type of situation, we can be certain of three things (a) they won't forget it (b) they will find a way to pay us back (c) we have little chance of getting their meaningful help or support in the future.

The Elegant Interruption

There is a whole other book in the cultural considerations around this activity. Some cultures *simply wouldn't dream* of interrupting. This is not the resource to outline which cultures those are, because there are plenty of online resources which can help, and we need to focus on the remote environment context. What is certain is that there will be times when we need to interrupt a conversation or contribution, and I am particularly interested in how to do this well at a distance. So, for the record, I appreciate that if we can see the other person, there are some visual and non-verbal strategies that can be used to signal our appetite for wanting to contribute to the conversation. Leaning in, looking at the person speaking, nodding, and opening your mouth as if you want to speak are all very effective ways of signaling your intent to contribute.

Our challenge is exacerbated when we can't see people. Think about what all too often happens. We are on a conference call where we cannot be seen and one of our colleagues is talking and talking and talking. So, what happens next? Usually (with the mute is on), the language disintegrates, and the hand gestures start. Or, we simply zone out and decide to return once again to our love affair with emails and start typing. Or, we wait until we are so frustrated, and then crash into the conversation where our emotion is audible. As a result, tension increases, rapport reduces and all the way around it simply doesn't work. If we want to convey impact and have presence remotely, this is undoubtedly a skillset that needs to be practised to become proficient.

Before sharing the technique, there is a really important concept that underpins it. Steven Covey's *'Seven Habits Of Highly Effective People'*[13] speaks to this framework. It is a metaphor of course, and effectively what it suggests is that rapport is like a bank account. You need to make deposits to increase it and withdrawals to reduce it. I have spoken about this elsewhere in the book, so we may be nodding now. So, what exactly do we need to do to interrupt elegantly?

Like most of the best verbal contributions, it is structured in three parts:

1. **State Their Name:** The first sound that we learn, but not necessarily the first word that we speak is our name. It creates a hard-wired response in us, and if you think about it, whenever we hear our own name, even when it is not meant for us, the sound causes us to stop and pause. Still not convinced? Then think about cats, dogs and horses. Whilst they may not be able to debate the pros and cons of a free market economy, they definitely understand the sound that is their name, and that when we say it; we are talking to them. However, let's get back to humans. Tonality is important when interrupting. It needs to be positive, neutral and without a shred of negative emotion.

2. **State Who You Are And What You've Done:** Good standard practice is to state your name so as to advise the audience who is speaking. However, what's really, really important is to demonstrate self-awareness at this exact

point. In other words, to recognise publicly what we have done; that being to interrupt. The reason for this is that we have made a withdrawal from their emotional bank account by interrupting them. So, in order for this not to be seen as eminently hostile or aggressive, it is vital to acknowledge what we have done.

3. **Make An Investment:** I'm talking about investing in their emotional bank account, and what we say should start with a power word: the word 'because'. 'Because' is a word that has extraordinary impact and I've explained why referencing Robert Cialdini's excellent book *Influence: The Psychology of Persuasion*[14], earlier in this chapter. The success of different types of interruption was linked to the word 'because'. Now back to making an investment in their emotional bank account. This could be by saying 'you've made a really good point that I want to talk more about'. Or, 'this is important to explore, so I have a question', or 'this is relevant to me, so I think that....' Or, 'this is the right area to emphasise, and we need to discuss it'. These are just examples, and obviously, we can't say the same thing every time. It's about developing a number of elegant verbal 'investment statements' so that when we complete our interruption, it happens effortlessly, easily and without causing lasting damage to the relationship or to the value of the conversation.

Sounds easy doesn't it? Well, in theory yes. However, the impact, and the difficulty, is in the execution. Again, again, again it takes practice.

Pacing And Leading

There is much that has been written on the psychology of influence. My background is in NLP (Neuro Linguistic Programming), which is all about understanding how we process information and then how that converts into the language we use to communicate with others. There is a technique called 'pacing and leading' that I specifically use with my clients to articulate their message when they need to disagree. The premise is simple, that being if I am going to disagree with you, and critically for you to be 'okay' with that, I need to build rapport whilst I am doing so. Yes, to actually *deepen rapport* rather than doing the opposite. The reality is that the reason why we often avoid disagreeing with others is precisely because of our fear that it will *damage rapport*. The distinction is that we need to *respond* to the perspective of others, rather than *react* to it. When we respond, it shows that we are listening; when we react, it shows that we're judging and potentially attacking. So, this means that we need to communicate firstly that we hear the other person and that we understand what they're saying. Remember, that's not the same as agreeing. Think about it for a moment, when we have a row with others, hopefully not colleagues and hopefully not very often in our personal life, then we certainly don't bother with any of this. What we do is continually assert our point of view, wrapped around a high level of emotion.

So, back to pacing and leading. There is some verbal and non-verbal (if possible) mirroring which is needed first. This is looking, sounding and being similar to each other and no mean feat to achieve. Think about when we watch the world go by in a coffee shop. We can just see those people who are connected, engaged, in rapport with each other in some way and that's what I'm talking about first of all. I've written about this elsewhere in the book, as well as in other my other books, so in the first instance, I'm simply saying this has got to be in play before we try to disagree without being disagreeable. And I don't underestimate the difficulty in achieving that.

The Constructive Challenge

I like to call it 'disagreeing without being disagreeable', and it is hard enough to do when we can literally see the whites of the eyes of our colleagues. However, it takes on a whole new level of difficulty when we cannot. My view is that there can be a reticence to challenge or disagree sufficiently in business and within teams as it is. Whilst there may be some cultural implications for certain parts of the world who do not tend towards constructive challenge, in general the reason why I think that many professionals step back from disagreeing is because we do not know how to do it *effectively*. In other words, we don't know how to protect and respect the relationship even when we don't respect or want to protect the point of view.

I have been working with a client in the oil and gas industry recently where the culture is direct, fast paced, with big characters doing extremely high value deals. This is not a cliché. It's just a business. However, the reason for my working with some leaders in this sector is because there is an inability to amend the behaviours necessary to drive results at the plants, suppliers and partners, and flex them to those needed to successfully influence across a global, matrix, corporate structure.

So, what do we then say? How do we structure our intervention for impact? Not surprisingly, I talk about crafting a contribution in three parts. Specifically:

1. Show that you've heard what they have said
2. Show that you understand what they have said
3. Use the word 'and' to connect (1) and (2) to the statement that we disagree

Do not use the word 'but' because of the reasons I explained earlier in this chapter. Follow the statement of disagreement with the word *because*. Remember 'because' is a power word that has enormous capacity to influence the perspectives of others as it links (a) a point of view/request/statement to (b) the reason for it. Finally, we need to state the reason why we disagree. The point is like much around communication, the theory is easy, the practice of *demonstrating it* is the bit that is much more tricky.

Pros And Cons

Given that we're talking about challenging constructively, I'm a big fan of offering options. Another strategy is 'pros and cons' where we can position our perspective within a context of balance. Often in business there are no easy, obvious answers. It's a war of attrition where we need to find the nuance that makes our recommended approach the most compelling. We need to show that we have heard what others are saying, understand the situation and are able to then influence through implicit or explicit deduction. 'Pros and Cons' is a very simple and effective way to demonstrate this, and hence garner support.

By way of illustration, "the pros of moving the project back by six weeks are that we will get more productivity, enhanced consumer insights and an important new hire on board. The cons are that it will cost an extra £100,000, mean that we miss our quarter end target and create a huge financial penalty for one of biggest customers. Given that our client is currently the biggest potential new investor in this technology, I suggest we close out now and deliver value to the account with what we have achieved so far." This is a very powerful way of framing the argument before making our recommendation.

The psychology of influence says that this is a strategy that allows us to demonstrate contrast. We are brought up with contrast (e.g. 'yes and no', 'ups and downs', 'left and right', 'old and new' etc.) It is extremely effective.

Building A Persuasive Argument

How do we win an argument without *having* an argument? My personal view is that the hardest challenge with influence is when we have to convince someone whose position is the complete opposite of our own. If we were to add into the mix that we really don't like them as a person, then we have a lot of work to do. So, how do we build a persuasive argument that enables us to get them onside and without damaging the relationship? How do we create and present a position which is different to our own, without appearing aggressive or confrontational? I have reflected on my findings at length and am particularly drawn to some strategies which I observe in the *most persuasive leaders.*

1. Be clear and logical with evidence: often having several sources of data helps.
2. Be relevant: stick to the essence of the argument and avoid being side-tracked on matters which are less important, or peripheral to the key point.
3. Be prepared: by this I mean anticipate around what issues others will challenge and rehearse counter points.
4. Go further: by this I mean in understanding the rationale for our argument. Why are we right? What are the reasons for this? Continue to delve into this, because effective debaters can draw threads across arguments that make it almost impossible for others to defeat.
5. Be the voice of the customer or the competitor: by this I mean if we have data that reflects what our customers say, or our competition say or do, then this is extremely powerful.
6. Be 'plugged in': by this I mean by identifying best in class practices, perhaps some of which are outside of our industry, that will support our argument. This strategy demonstrates our strategic approach and has the added bonus of being proven to work.
7. Be forensic about finding the gaps: by this I mean finding the weaknesses in the opposing argument and having clear commentary to address them.

8. Don't do 'yes/but': because that always riles. It's also what we did as children when we argued. Listen to the alternative perspective, acknowledge it but not agree with it and show we've heard it.

9. Keep it short: lengthy answers rarely persuade. Be crisp, be concise and be compelling. This is far punchier and far more effective.

10. Be neutral in tone: by this I mean vocal tone and it is essential in a remote environment. Anger, sarcasm, frustration, impatience increases the tension in the discussion. Remaining neutral, even if others do not, will greatly enhance our credibility and influence.

11. Be prepared to concede on some points. We don't have to be right about absolutely everything with our argument to be able to persuade others to agree with it.

Wins And Learns

Another approach to communicating a balanced perspective is 'wins and learns'. The difference in terms of 'pros and cons' is subtle in that it is evidential (i.e. based on what has already happened), versus pros and cons, which is based on what we might choose to do in the future.

The Pivot

Quite simply this is the ability to be agile to the needs of our audience and flexible in the moment regarding how we communicate with them. It is predicated on a further ability, that being to be able to read the room and realise that our message is not landing. These are two distinct skills and I do not underestimate the challenge being able to do *them both.* Remember that reading the room is challenging even when we are in it and can see, hear and feel what is happening. At a distance, through the prism of technology, with perhaps with a time delay and potentially not being able to see the other person, makes for a much more challenging level of complexity.

Assuming that we are able to gauge that our communication isn't working, then remember the mantra: 'the quality of our communication is in the response it gets'. There may be a number of different reasons why we might need to pivot, including:

- *Our communication style.* There are many different assessment tools, and no doubt dear reader you have completed a number of them over the course of your career to date that indicate your own preferences around how you communicate. Do you tend to make statements or ask questions? Do you tend to show emotion or conceal it? Are you task focused or relationship focused in your message? Do you say a lot or say a little? Do you tend to speak first or tend to speak last in a group? The list goes on and on and it's important to stress that there are no right and wrong communication styles. Quite simply the important point is of course that our communication styles are different and we are more open to be influenced by people whose typical communication style is very similar to that of our own. So, we need to be able to flex our style to suit our audience, and the individual members of it, when engaged 1:1, in order to be persuasive and compelling.

- *How informed our audience are.* A classic example is one that I find myself working often with my clients to address. They are bright, smart, successful leaders with a great deal of often technical knowledge. If we are technical experts and we're talking to other technical experts; then talking all things technical is typically absolutely fine. We do not need to pivot because both parties can speak the language. However, if our audience is not comprised of technical specialists then our droning on and on with our detailed, technical language will confuse, frustrate and distract. We need to be able to move from the language of our expertise to the language of soundbites, simplicity and brevity. By so doing, we are not patronising our audience. Far from it. We are demonstrating the requirement to flex and the ability to convert one message into something which makes sense and which engages others.

- *The seniority of the group*: senior leaders want to hear a story. They want a crisp, concise, compelling message that is easily grasped and clearly set in a commercial and strategic context. Getting to the point fast, without all the background regarding how we got here, and without sharing all the data to prove each point is key. If they want to scrutinise what we recommend, then trust me, they will do.

- *Competing and varied priorities*: Being able to put the same message in a different context to fit the priorities of the listener requires us to be able to pivot. We can be recommending exactly the same thing, but the reasons *why* it makes sense may be different, based on differing priorities. So, I call this the ability to move from *what* to *why* with fluidity and ease.

- *The receptivity of the audience*: Communicating a message when the audience is benign and supportive is one thing, being able to challenge and defend our position when the audience is skeptical at best, is quite another. To be effective we need to be concise, speak directly and immediately to their issues and concerns and remain positive and optimistic in our tone.

- *The amount of time available*: We have all been there; the plan was to have a full thirty minutes to discuss our idea and we've just been told that due to an already overrunning agenda this has now been truncated to a mere five minutes. One of the activities that I run with my clients is called '3/30/3'. Essentially this is an activity that is based on being able to tell messages of varying lengths. So, think 3 minutes, 30 seconds, 3 words. It is the same thing when making a verbal contribution. We aren't warned in advance how much time we have; we only know the we have lost the audience when they cut us off, interrupt us to say we're running out of time and have to wrap up now etc.

Making A Contribution That Counts

Part of being an effective communicator is being an effective listener and ready to make a contribution with little opportunity to prepare. I was working recently with a client where my role was to observe their contributions. One of the Supply Chain specialists was asked a question. In essence it was his opinion which was being sought. Unfortunately, he started speaking and simply never stopped.

Whilst I am certain that I was not the only individual in the room who was, at one level, genuinely enjoying his witty anecdotes as they tumbled forth, merging into a stream of rapid-fire consciousness. At another level, I had simply no idea what he was really talking about in relation to work, much less be able to identify what I was supposed to do with what he was sharing. The length, the complexity, the diversity, the analogies of his monologue simply overwhelmed me, as well as reminded me of the *necessity* in ensuring that when we open our mouths, be it face-to-face or remotely, *we need to make contributions that count.*

So, picture the scene. You are on a teleconference or telepresence. You have an opportunity to speak. It's your big moment and the audience is waiting. The 'virtual floor' is yours. It is a 'lights, camera, action' moment on the remote call. And then what happens? We completely mess it up. Either because:

- We have forgotten what we were going to say.
- We get distracted whilst speaking and we all know that doesn't end well.
- We weren't really listening because the phone was on mute and we were busy cranking out those emails. However now we need to say something, which we do, but which doesn't add value because someone else has already said it.
- We haven't rehearsed the essence of our message.
- We waffle on and on until the end of time and until someone can stand it no longer and interrupts us.
- We provide an answer which is actually so short that there follows a stunned and slightly awkward silence. It sounded much better in our head than it did out loud.
- Or for some other reason that I've not listed. The point is that we've all been there.

Contributions that count avoid everything listed so far, and they achieve exactly what the moniker suggests. A critical first point is that *thinking about* what we want to say **is very different to the experience of actually saying it.** So, two points in that: the structure and the rehearsal. Let's talk about structure first:

- **Divide our message into 3 parts:** Like all good stories, a great message should be divided into three parts. Why three? Well, ask an engineer and they will talk about how the triangle is the strongest structure because of how it enables weight to be borne. Ask an anthropologist and they will say that humans and animals look to create familiarity and certainty in their world and that means creating patterns. A pattern occurs with not one data point, because it's a singular point, not two data points, because that creates contrast, but in actual fact with three data points. Ask a storyteller and they will say that if you get this narrative structure right first, then it is much easier to get the amount of detail right afterwards. If we start in the hopeful expectation that we will just 'work it out as we go along'…. all I can say is by way of reply: 'good luck with that'.

- **Be concise:** Avoid long contributions. We all work in an attention deficit economy and particularly if you are on a T-con and so can't see the reaction of others, then the danger of 'over speaking' is much higher. We need to listen to verbal cues of our audiences, such as sighs, attempted interruptions, verbal nods or shakes, all of which are powerful signals not to be ignored.
- **Be consistent with energy:** In other words, don't trail off towards the end of our contribution. Our cadence, tempo and emotion should be the same throughout.
- **Be relevant:** Make our contribution *blatantly obvious* in terms of how it connects to the conversation. It has to add value and *must not* repeat that which at least three other people have already shared.
- **Finish with a flourish**, and that means the same amount of energy and momentum with which we started. Think about it like our verbal 'full stop.' Avoid trailing off because this simply isn't impactful and sounds literally and metaphorically like we have run out of steam. It will be the last verbal image that we convey; so, make it count.

What To Say When You Don't Know What To Say

There are some specific strategies that can be very effective when we find ourselves in a scenario where we need to share an answer when either (a) there isn't an easy one (b) our opinion isn't fully formed yet (c) we want to make a contribution without being too definitive (d) saying 'I don't know' isn't an option on this particular occasion for whatever reasons of political sensitivity.

A Word Of Warning

Before we go any further, it's really important to strike a note of caution. If the strategies outlined below become our default approach to making verbal contributions when we are communicating remotely, then beware. We will frustrate, irritate and infuriate our colleagues and achieve the complete opposite of that which we might have intended. In other words, these strategies need care and selective deployment in order to be successful. A great example of where this is used to excess is with politicians. If you listen to any political chat show for any length of time then these can be heard, repeatedly. All too often the audience becomes alienated, disenfranchised and dismissive. We're not aiming to achieve that as an outcome.

What is certainly true in terms of structure for these verbal strategies is that, like any good story, they all share a common theme. We know the drill by now, split the answer into three parts.

Perspective

The intent here is to answer in three parts with the structure of our message being based around perspective. Perspective means point of view. Imagine being asked the following question on a conference call: *'what do you think is our greatest strength as a business?'* This question is purely to illustrate the approach. In this example, we could answer the question by structuring our commentary as if we were a customer, then as a shareholder and finally, as an employee. The 'why should we bother with this?' question is a reasonable one to ask. The point is that with questions such as these, there are no 'right' answers; just our point of view. When we are not comfortable or willing to be definitive, it's one way to structure any answer that can convey thoughtfulness and credibility.

Time

This is a different way to answer the same question. Again if the question is *'what do you think is our greatest strength as a business?'* However the structure of the answer is different. For example: "historically I would say it's our expertise in working with the car industry, currently it's our project management capability and in the future, I think it will be how we are responding to the challenge of digital disruption." The structure of our answer remains in three parts, however we have organised it using a different framework.

Geography

My hope is that we are starting to get the point. These are just examples of ways to structure an answer and in this instance, it's about 'place'. Using the same question answered a different way might be "in Japan the answer is customer service, in Europe it's the sales team and in the USA our engineering capability is our greatest strength".

People

Once more, it is still the same question, but this time the answer could be focused around (a) literally three different people. So, in answer to the question *'what do you think is our greatest strength as a business?'* it is possible to structure an answer around people. "If you ask Bob, he'll say X, if you ask Tony, he'll say Y and if you ask Fred, he'll say Z".

Of course, there are a number of different examples of a narrative structure, the point is that these frameworks help to organise our answer. It remains a great verbal tool with significant application and I encourage us all to explore how it can help us.

Things We Don't Like Saying – But Sometimes Have To

One of the least liked phrases in business to say is 'I don't know'. So, first strategy is to know how to say 'I don't know' with confidence and authority, rather than saying 'I don't know' with apology and embarrassment. Tonality, pace and articulation is important. Other examples of things we don't like saying might include 'I'm sorry', 'you're right; I'm wrong' etc. The point is that unless we get the vocal tone right then not only can we dance around the issue which is obvious to everyone else on the call, but also we run the distinct risk of sounding absurd.

Saying 'No'

Saying no isn't easy. We worry about the consequences of doing so and as a result, can easily waffle on and on forever with tedious and unnecessary attempts to soften the blow. Sometimes I am reminded of clumsy efforts to end a relationship, with the attendant 'it's not you it's me' nonsense. Lengthy, rambling excuses prevail which no-one on either side really believes. To have impact requires us to simply use the word itself, and then in a clear and concise fashion, articulate the reason why. I talk elsewhere in this book about the word 'because'. It is a power word. We need to say 'no', use the word 'because' to explain why and keep it brief. Sometimes we don't even need an explanation, it's simply a 'no'. Vocal tonality is important here yet again. Avoiding the high rising terminal is essential; in other words, the vocal tone rising at the end of sentences, because this dramatically reduces the effect of what we need to say. Instead of sounding definitive, we sound uncertain. Instead of sounding confident, we sound unsure. Instead of being able to demonstrate gravitas, we convey hesitancy and weakness. We need to ensure that our vocal tone is either neutral or drops at the end of a sentence. By adopting all these tips, when we say 'no' we sound like we believe it and our audience are far more likely to be persuaded by, and not offended by it.

Saying 'I Don't Know'

This is an extraordinarily common challenge for leaders, and it is worth taking a moment to explore why. If we think about the early stages of our career, the focus is on building technical competence and skills in our functional area and market segment. We acquire knowledge, build capability and learn a lot. However, for all leaders there comes a point when it's not about knowing everything. Why? *Because we lead teams of people who we've hired to know the detail and on whom we rely for their specific, granular expertise.* As our remit gets larger, as the size of the organisation we run expands, it is simply not possible to be all over every detail. I am minded to repeat a well-worn cockney expression which I have mentioned elsewhere and works perfectly here. It is simply this: "*you don't have a dog and bark yourself*".

The other piece that I believe feeds into understanding why saying '*I don't know*' is so difficult is when we fear exposure and judgment for incompetence. At the time of writing this book, I have been working with a global business in the oil and gas field. One of their operational rhythms is where senior leaders fly into a region to scrutinise the performance of the business and the leaders who run it. Part of their role is to challenge, stretch and extend thinking around leaders' performance and strategy, and my view is that if a senior leader is doing a great job, *they should* ask questions to which their direct reports might not always know the answer. It is almost counter intuitive to then suggest to leaders that they need to get comfortable and confident with saying '*I don't know*'.

And yet we all need to be good at this.

Being a persuasive and credible leader means being able to convey confidently and positively and answer that is "I don't know", rather than falling into the trap of talking a lot of nonsense. The plain truth is this: if we don't know the answer to a question, *the majority of the time the audience will work out that we don't know.* Lengthy, irrelevant waffle is easily identified for being just that; and it damages our brand and our credibility. There is far more confidence and authority to be had when we readily admit we don't know, and remain positive and action oriented about what we are going to do about it.

A final note is this: what I am *not* suggesting is that it's okay to 'not know' a lot of things. I am *not saying* that if we show up to a senior leader review meeting, or investors call or customer meeting and convey that we don't know a lot of things that this is acceptable. *Clearly it is not*. Do not mistake my comments for being unprepared, slack or lazy. What I am saying is that sometimes we don't know the answer and that's okay. How we communicate our response when we don't know matters. Appearing faltering or embarrassed isn't great. We should pause, consider our response and then be optimistic, action oriented in what we say. Finally as a foot note, leadership integrity stands or falls by our 'say/do' ratio. If we say we're going to find out, get more detail on an issue or take more control, then *we absolutely have to do so.* If we don't, then we get what we deserve the next time this topic comes up and, we've damaged our own leadership brand.

Admitting That We Didn't Deliver The Result

Now this really isn't easy. However, if we don't work out how to do it well then we can expect to be pilloried. I work with many different sales leaders across a number of organisations and industries. The plain and simple truth is that we don't always deliver performance. However, when faced with the scrutiny of the business, it's all too easy and understandable to become defensive. I totally understand why, and yet it does us no favours because it damages our credibility and reduces our trustworthiness. We need to articulate what we have learned, where we have failed, how we will be different and what support we need. Speaking as an ex-national sales leader myself, there were times whereas a team we nailed the number, and there were times when frankly we did not.

We cannot have it both ways. In other words when it is all going great, we say it is down to the team and what we did; and yet when we didn't deliver, it was because of the market, the competition, our colleagues, the unreasonableness of the client and so on. All leaders, whether they are in sales or not, are held accountable to metrics of performance. When we fail, our role is to craft the story that says:

- Why We Didn't Deliver

- What We Have Learned
- What Will Be Different Moving Forward

There are many different narrative structures that will work. Another is:

- What We Have Changed
- How That Will Impact Performance
- What You Can Expect In The Future

Our language and our delivery have to be straightforward, not defensive, pragmatic and optimistic. It also has to be focused on what we can control and avoid finger pointing - even if the collateral we did get from Marketing was worse than useless. It doesn't matter. We need to rehearse and deliver the story convincingly, take responsibility for underperformance and acknowledge the criticism or disappointment of others.

The Perfect Question

In a remote environment, if we're going to make useful contributions to drive the conversation forward, one skill set that we absolutely have to master is the skill of questioning. The difference between managers and leaders as far as I can tell is that managers have all the right answers and leaders have all the right questions. As a coach, whilst this is one of the tools of our trade, effective use of crisp questioning is a pet peeve of mine. Wherever we turn, there are many examples of how dreadfully this is done. Great questions should stretch our thinking, pause the madness, encourage us to explore new possibilities, check our facts, explore our expertise – amongst many other things. Clear, crisp, concise questions, and asked one at a time, are the way forward here. If we want to understand how *not* to do it, then listen to a political interview or radio show. The ability of journalists to ask multiple questions at the same time, intersperse a question with an opinion, repeat the question in three different ways and generally ask lengthy, irrelevant, waffle and nonsense is extraordinary.

The perfect question must be open, concise with a clear objective in asking it. Taking a moment to understand what exactly we want to achieve by posing a question, along with 'shutting up' as soon as we have asked it *are absolutely essential*. I invite my clients to create a list of 'killer' questions that represent their

Sarah Brummitt

favourite, 'go-to' questions when looking to explore an issue, add value, scrutinize, challenge, debate and progress issues. Examples include:

- What are we trying to achieve?
- Why are we doing this?
- What if we did nothing?
- Why do this *now?*
- What's the worst thing that can happen?
- What works well?
- What if anything were possible?
- What do our customers want?
- Who can we learn from?
- Who is better at this than we are?
- What organisations are addressing this issue most successfully?
- How are our competition handling this?
- How do we take cost and complexity out of this?
- What next?
- Who's doing what now?

By no means are these a definitive list. The point is that it is about having a list of open, powerful, thought provoking questions that are designed to move the conversation forward, shift perspective, kill bad ideas early, get to a decision and so on. They are not designed to be asked just for the sake of it, however if they are effective, we should find ourselves using them quite a lot.

The Problem With Questions

Is that they represent multiple opportunities to get it wrong, and when we do, our verbal impact is massively reduced. Here are some of the most common mistakes:

- Asking multiple questions at once. For example: *'What is your view on this? Do you think it will be a success? And how will you make sure that we remain within our budget?'* I call this 'question stacking'. Usually the most important is the first question we ask; however all too often it is the last question that will be answered by our audience.

- Intertwining our opinion into a question. For example: *'How are we going to do this? Because I think there are a number of issues here around bandwidth. I know for a fact that in Europe they are going to be slower than elsewhere in getting go so perhaps we should leave Denmark and Sweden out of this'.* It is harder to understand the construct of our question and others might disengage because they didn't realise the question really needed answering. This is because what we have simultaneously shared is a lengthy discourse of our opinion, and the audience has either forgotten what we asked them, or no longer cares.

- Not listening carefully to others *in order* to be able to ask great questions. In other words, we have our own agenda of questions and we are going to crash on with it, whether or not they are the most useful or relevant questions to be asking anymore. Remember the mantra, not only do great leaders have great questions, but so also do great *influencers.*

So, we've covered a lot of ground in this chapter. I would encourage us all to think about where we need to enhance our remote presence by making more impactful verbal contributions. Then choose the strategies to use and practise, practise, practise until we are fluent and effective at them.

Chapter Nine – Other Things We Must Do To Convey Remote Presence

This is a 'catch all' chapter for 'dos' and 'don'ts' which fail to readily sit elsewhere within the book, or, which I have alluded to in the context of yet something else we need to be good at if we are to convey remote presence. However, they are important because failing to execute well will impact our ability to be perceived as an effective remote communicator. A final note, I've split this out to reflect the scenario where (a) it's our remote meeting and we're running it (b) we're attending a remote meeting. Yes, there is some deliberate consistency across both groups; however, there are also some differences and the way I've written this book is to make it easy for the reader to jump to the sections which are most relevant to them.

If We're Running A Remote Meeting

Be Prepared

I've written about this elsewhere and make no apology for some repetition here. We should:

- Open up the call early (fifteen minutes) to allow people to join, resolve any technical issues and do some small talk. This matters! We don't walk straight into a room when we meet face-to-face and immediately sit down and get straight on with business. We need time to connect, reduce social tension and increase rapport. It's our job to facilitate that. Remember, irrespective of the industry in which we work, we are all in the relationship industry.
- Check our equipment so our headset, back up batteries for remote keyboards and mousepads, ensure our camera and volume levels work well.
- Update our software; all too often time is wasted because we have not checked that the software provider has issued an update, and it will take twenty minutes on a slow broadband signal to download.

Show Initiative On The Use Of Technology

For example:

- Remind the audience of different elements of platform functionality (views, camera and microphone functions, chat, hand up, whiteboards, polls, breakout rooms etc.)

- Ask people to put their cameras on and mute their microphones if not engaged in the conversation.
- To avoid the 'talking over' challenge, explain under the 'process' part of the '3 Ps' strategy (and if you don't know what that is, go back to Chapter Seven and take a look), and how to overcome it. The use of 'hand up' and chat functions are two really effective strategies to help in the remote meeting world.
- Remind the audience of different elements of functionality as we move through the meeting in order to make the most of it and avoid people becoming disengaged because they forgot what we said at the start or weren't listening properly the first time.

Stick To Time

Another pet peeve of mine are meetings which are scheduled to start at a certain time and then don't because we're waiting for the ever fragrant Bob to get a grip and get on the call (after he's got his coffee, got a life, got a decent internet connection etc.) Always start on time because it shows respect for others. Equally *always end on time too*. We are much more likely to do this if we have clarity on our purpose for the conversation and exercised outstanding chairmanship skills. So, if this currently our experience, revisit where I talk about both earlier in the book and identify where we need to start developing the skills.

Avoid Lazy Habits Regarding Remote Meeting Length

Does our meeting *really* need to last an hour? Or even thirty minutes? I have alluded to this elsewhere, and I repeat the necessity to scrutinize the start and finish times as well as the length of our meetings. Global digital brands schedule ten-minutes or fifteen-minutes meetings, and get a lot done during that time. If we think about the occasions where the first ten minutes of a meeting have been wasted waiting for stragglers, then we had internet connection challenges and had to drop off and dial in, then we couldn't hear our friend Bob, then we went around the houses for twenty minutes because it was clear people hadn't done their prep, then we got stuck in a vortex for a while because another Bob took over and no-one stopped him etc. etc. Again, this is just nonsense. We need to build a brand as being a leader who runs short, targeted, outcome driven remote meetings where decisions get made and actions get agreed by those who show up. We will soon start changing how people approach our conference calls and telepresence sessions and believe me, if they care, they will be on time and ready to talk.

Achieve Your Objective

Or give us a damn good reason why today we did not. We are on remote calls to make decisions, agree actions and make commitments. We are *not* on remote calls to have discussions, cover agendas and then agree to meet again to have more discussions and cover more agendas. Discussions and agendas are the means by which we achieve our end goal, namely our objective. As leaders, sometimes we need to be agile and change from what was planned, however our rationale for so doing must be crystal clear, otherwise our audience does not engage with it. Being influential remotely means building a brand as someone who runs efficient meetings that stay on time and clearly achieve what they were set out to achieve.

Offer Help

There's a fantastic quote that I have paraphrased from Brené Brown[43] that is effectively this: 'get on the pitch, roll up your sleeves and stop moaning from the cheap seats'. My point is simple: it's really easy to criticise and, there are times when, of course, it is necessary. However, in the long run, our ability to be influential will wane over time because our stakeholders will become defensive, disregard our input and ultimately want to keep us out of decisions and conversations. Our brand will become the 'mood hoover' or doom monger in the group. This should never be an aspiration, not least because we work in a business world that relies on co-operation and collaboration. So, good luck with getting their help when we need it further down the track. A far better strategy is to focus on offering help, ideas, suggestions that might work, a willingness to either get involved personally, or leverage our network to connect others who could help. To be clear, I am not suggesting we're always trying to do everyone's work for them, but what I am suggesting is that we should adopt an approach that is ultimately 'how can we fix this?' rather than 'I'm having fun doing nothing but criticise and I am not going to lift a finger'. There is a difference.

Follow Up In A Timely Fashion

This is just good meeting etiquette, and especially as part of the rhythm of regular events which we might hold with our teams. If we made decisions, agreed commitments and took action, then let's follow up to see what that delivered in terms of value.

Review Remote Meeting Activity Regularly

My research revealed that this is particularly important when we have a recurring rhythm of meetings. One of my clients is in the telecommunications sector and I have had the pleasure of working with leaders from across the value chain over the years. A senior Account Director expressed enormous frustration at being expected to attend a relatively operational level service update meeting every week. He wasn't offering value and made very little contributions in the three hour (!) session. Now, we can explore how part of his growth as a leader was in empowering and enabling his team to have the confidence to carry on without him, but in any event, this situation also reveals our need when hosting meetings to regularly review and ensure we have the right people in the virtual room to fully participate in the right conversations. It's all too easy to let these linger on the calendar, have dwindling attendees and a growing sense that it is all a bit of a waste of time. We need to take the initiative, review effectiveness regularly and change accordingly.

Invite Others To Our Meetings And Hit Two Birds With One Stone

We should build our network continually and strategically as a successful professional and this particular strategy is an incredibly effective way to do it. Our remote meetings should be an opportunity to learn, be curious, ask questions, develop our expertise and increase our confidence. One way to do that is by inviting leaders from across the organization, and outside of it, who can educate us, inspire us, develop us, inform us. We learn a lot, we make new contacts and we better understand (if we're strategic about it), how to influence them in the future. This *is not* about 'filling time'; it's about being smart in continuing to grow and continuing to build better relationships with those whom we need to influence.

If We're Attending A Meeting

There are some things we need to do well to be influential. My word of warning here is that *very often* the cultural norm pushes back on a number of these strategies. Don't become part of it. Leaders with presence, in this case remotely, stand out for doing the right things, rather than blend in with everyone else for doing the wrong ones.

Some Easy Wins

As I have researched this book and attended and led countless remote meetings, there are some things that I didn't think I would have to write; but I will reiterate their importance once more for two reasons (a) because we may have missed where I commented on them elsewhere in this book and (b) because I have encountered them repeatedly being missed by professionals and as a result, their remote presence is dramatically impeded:

- We must always make an effort with what we wear and grooming
- Never do a remote call whilst sitting on our bed, with our headboard in the background and visible
- If we absolutely have to do a remote call on our phone with our camera switched on, invest in a stand, so that it can be static
- Don't move around with our mobile phone camera turned on, because it visually very dramatic for the audience and is not a good look for us
- Don't message with our camera turned on, particularly if using a mobile phone because all the audience sees are our fingers across the lens as we tap away. Again, it doesn't look good and raises the issue of our engagement with the meeting.

The Basic Courtesies Matter

Be on time. We manage our time; no one else does. It is our responsibility and how we manage it tells the world what we care about. If we're late to a meeting it's because we are either (a) disorganised (b) disinterested (c) unable to assert our needs in the context of other meetings or conversations that were happening right before the remote call we should be joining. In any event, it is our fault and our responsibility to fix it. Being late once can happen to all of us. Being late twice is unfortunate. Being late three times is a pattern and one that we have choice to address, or choose not to. But to be clear: it is our choice. Being respectful of others' time, which is as important as our own, is a small but *incredibly important* courtesy to pay them, and we should be consistent in doing it. It shows a deposit in their emotional bank account and no matter what the culture of our business, we should always be on time.

Be Visible

It's not a win to think 'wow, I've just cranked out thirty emails whilst those losers were droning on for the last hour on that conference call, plus I've done my online grocery shopping and had a good catch up with a friend.' Being a leader means being visible, and not for the sake of it, but rather in order to make contributions which driver higher value discussions, better decisions and more productive action. If we don't know why we are on the call, if the objectives are not clear, or if we think it is in fact a pointless waste of everyone's time, then this is an opportunity *to influence and lead.* Talk to the meeting organiser ahead of the session to discuss and clarify. Note that I've deliberately used the word *'talk'*. In this instance, a discussion is far more likely to have impact and drive a mutually beneficial outcome than sending an email which could be ignored or misinterpreted. Leadership doesn't happen by invitation, it happens when we identify opportunities to create change, offer help, improve processes, problems and performance and we need to take ownership for doing so and make it happen. What we should not do is fall into the trap of finding shortcuts, such as making one comment at the beginning then zoning out, or making a couple of comments on a chat function just to show we are still there on the call. This is all just nonsense, and if we think that others don't realise what we're doing then we are kidding no-one but ourselves.

Do Your Homework

It sounds like leadership 101 to say show up prepared. However there's a subtlety to this which is easily missed. I'm talking about being prepared regarding the key messages that we want to convey during the conversation. *Thinking* about what we want to say *is completely different to actually saying it.* Therefore rehearsal is very important. Throughout the three years of research that I have completed for this book, what I observed repeatedly was a distinct different between those leaders who were fluent and persuasive, especially under pressure, versus those who were not.

That difference was preparation and rehearsal. There is a very big difference between the cognitive process of *thinking about* what we want to say and the mechanical process *of saying it*. We can't work it out in the moment, because we'll stumble and we will not be anywhere near as persuasive.

Ask Intelligent Questions

I talk often about being able to ask the right question, in the right way, at the right time to shift perspective, challenge others, focus discussion, drive decisions, agree actions and get commitment. Open, relevant, concise, thought provoking questions are the way forward. They aren't readily conjured out of thin air if we have not done our homework and are not listening closely to what is being discussed. This links to my earlier point about preparation. The old adage: fail to prepare; prepare to fail comes to mind here.

Have (The Right) High Impact Introduction Ready

One of the industries with which I have had the pleasure of gathering a lot of experience is the world of law. Like other sectors such as medicine, professional services, armed forces and so on, hierarchy is *everything*. They are not flat, matrix structures in the way that many other types of global business are. Why does this matter? It matters because the more junior members of a team are challenged to find their space in the conversation and what this can mean is that in group settings, whether it's face-to-face or remote, the numbers of opportunities to make contributions can be few. Don't misunderstand the comment as a slight or disrespectful. These are technically precise, highly experienced professionals where the reality is that the more senior team members naturally dominate airtime and this is expected because *"they are the Partner"*. Getting on and getting ahead is a competitive business, and even though a very junior member is not best qualified to comment on the more difficult technical aspects of a case, *this does not mean* that they can't create impact. Getting the introduction right is a good place to start.

Offer Help

It's not a 'win' to think, 'my goal for this call is to leave it without any action'. If so, why are we on the call? What's our value to this team and this conversation? What exactly are doing here? We can all, with reasonable legitimacy, claim to be too busy.

It is the same responsibility for an attendee that it is for the person who is running the meeting. Offers to support others in a practical sense are incredibly helpful, plus that help doesn't need to represent vast drains on our time. Making connections, sharing best practices or key information, offering ideas, giving a wider organisational, market or strategic perspective are all examples of how we can provide help and support that don't require a major drain on our budget or calendar. So, we need to ensure embrace this approach, otherwise we can reasonably expect others to adopt an unhelpful approach towards us, right when we need it most.

Avoid 'Getting On A Roll'

Have you noticed how it's very easy to wax lyrical about what *won't* work? I have observed repeated in remote conversations a peculiar trait of herd mentality, where momentum starts to gather around the negative. One person articulates a problem or challenge, which is perfectly appropriate and legitimate to do, then another person agrees and reiterates, then a third person weighs in with much the same point and so it goes on and on. Once the point is made, we need to pivot to the issue of how we will address the challenge, rather than use up acres of time repeating what's already been said and violently agreeing with each other. Being persuasive and influential balances a constructive critique of reality with a future focus, because the future is where we're all heading, whether we like it or not.

If There Was Pre-Reading......

Then we should read it, or at least look at it with some meaningful consideration for ten minutes. Clearly, if it was sent mere moments before the call then this does not apply, and, if it was not subsequently used or referenced then we should explore why this was the case. Again, this speaks to our willingness to want to step into leadership, rather than be a bystander to a situation that may on occasion, be less than perfect. In addition, we need to take responsibility for the fact that one of the reasons meetings drag on, leading to another meeting and then another meeting, is because there wasn't sufficient preparation done in the first place. In a number of instances, we could all ultimately save a lot of time if we just read the information in advance.

Invest In The 'Emotional Bank Account' Of Others

We can't influence people who don't trust us, it's as simple as that. The responsibility for an attendee is the same as the leader running the meeting when it comes to the 'emotional bank account' concept. Fundamentally all human beings go in to any interaction with the goal of leaving it with their self-worth intact and everyday out emotional bank account is set back to zero. Therefore, we need to make deposits in order to create connection, increase rapport and most importantly, build trust. How do we this? A myriad of different ways. Look at people (most professionals don't know how to do that on remote calls, so revisit other chapters in this book to understand how to do this effectively). In addition, name checking others, asking questions, showing appreciation, demonstrating courtesy, positively referencing them, head nodding when they speak, smiling (obviously we need to be on camera for that to have an impact), letting them finish speaking, are all examples of how we can effectively invest in others in order to build rapport.

Rehearse Key Messages

It is very easy to write all of these strategies down in a book, but without rehearsal we are unlikely to be effective when it really matters. I'm not suggesting that we have to rehearse each contribution in advance; that would be absurd. However, if we know we've got a tough message to share, or a challenging request to make and we also know that we're going to feel some energy around it; then we should rehearse it to ensure fluency and comfort.

Be A Chairman – Even If You're Not

We cannot always be certain that the person running the meeting has the chairmanship skills necessary to keep the conversation going in the right direction and at the right pace. So, help them out. Don't leave it to them to sort out and judge them when they fail. The reason for offering such a wide variety of chairmanship skills elsewhere in this book is to encourage *us* to do this when it is needed. That is adding real value and our colleagues will thank us later.

Chapter Ten – Using Slides Remotely

Many organisations and leaders use slides to support their message, and this makes our challenge even greater when it comes to being influential at a distance. Often the presenter and the audience have their cameras off, so that once again, it is an invisible audience, and the point of visual reference now becomes the slides. The potential for confusion, chaos, disinterest and disengagement is *enormous*. So, I have highlighted some of the most important strategies to using slides successfully in a remote environment, starting with how we build them.

Why Is Storytelling On Slides So Important?

Because historians, scientists, engineers and academics have argued for years that poor PowerPoint slides have led to a loss of life.

It was January 16th, 2003, and the NASA Mission led by the Space Shuttle Columbia was underway. Seven men and women left Earth with their objective being to study the effects of microgravity on the human body. Columbia had been the first Space Shuttle and had been on 27 missions prior to this one.

At the beginning, all was well. After the launch, the crew settled into their sixteen-day mission, however those back at Mission Control quickly realised that something had gone horribly wrong.

As a matter of protocol, NASA staff reviewed footage from an external camera mounted to the fuel tank. At eighty-two seconds into the launch, a piece of spray on foam insulation (SOFI) fell from one of the ramps that attached the shuttle to its external fuel tank. This piece of foam collided with one of the tiles on the outer edge of the shuttle's left wing, and whilst it was impossible to tell from Earth how much damage this foam, we should note that the velocity of such an event was the equivalent of a speed which is nine times faster than a fired bullet.

Foam falling during launch is apparently, nothing new. The same incident had happened on four previous missions and it was in fact, one of the reasons why the camera was there in the first place. Unfortunately, however, the tile the foam had struck was on the edge of the wing designed to protect the shuttle from the heat of Earth's atmosphere during launch and re-entry. In space the shuttle was safe, but

NASA didn't know how it would respond to re-entry. There were a number of options. The astronauts could perform a spacewalk and visually inspect the hull. NASA could launch another Space Shuttle to pick the crew up. Or they could risk re-entry.

NASA officials sat down with Boeing Corporation engineers who took them through three reports; a total of twenty-eight slides. The salient point was whilst there was data showing that the tiles on the shuttle wing could tolerate being hit by the foam. However, this was based on test conditions using foam more than 600 times *smaller than that which had struck Columbia*. The slide used to demonstrate this point was: well, ambiguous to say the least.

NASA listened to the engineers and their PowerPoint. The engineers felt they had communicated the potential risks very clearly. NASA believed that all data pointed to there not being enough damage to put the lives of the crew in danger. They rejected the other options and pushed ahead with Columbia re-entering Earth's atmosphere as normal, but as history tells us, Columbia and those on board were tragically lost.

Edward Tufte, a Professor at Yale University and expert in communication reviewed the slideshow the Boeing engineers had given NASA and found how the slide decks were presented was particularly significant to the decision-making process which unfolded. The complexity, density and ambiguity of their slides impacted the decision by NASA. How amazing is that?

Creating Persuasive Slide Decks

Do Our Homework

This means finding out about our audience in terms of their preferences for communication, how much detail they want to see, the type of information they will be persuaded by etc. Do they want detail in an appendix? Do they want the answer first? What's the goal for the slide deck anyway? If we are going to put together a slide deck, we will save ourselves a great deal of time and effort if we seek some clarity on this *first* before getting lost in PowerPoint.

Have Fewer Slides

Far too often professionals bring too many slides to the discussion. Five, three, maybe one slide? The debate isn't necessarily how low we can go on number, rather that we bring *the absolute minimum to make the case* in the time we have. A common reality in a remote environment is that we have far less time than we thought anyway, so bringing lots of slides makes absolutely no sense at all.

Honour The Principles Of A Story

Remember, a story is a structured message specifically designed to inspire and influence others. Hence, everything that we have talked elsewhere in this book regarding what makes a message a *story* really matters. Our decks should have a clear goal, a narrative structure, a hook, use metaphor and analogy appropriately, STAR moments and a clear 'ask'.

Remember The 'Peak End Rule'

This proven psychological construct shows that how we remember things is based heavily on two factors: (a) the most intense feeling we had during the experience (good or bad) and (b) the end of the experience. In the world of creating slides this is important because obviously there is an all too often associated bias that slides equate to boring. In addition, we need to 'end on a high'. All of the areas about which I've written earlier in the book *are absolutely critical*.

Resist Clever Technological Wizzardry

Tempting though it is to put videos, embedded files and lots of eye-popping animation, my recommendation is: beware. Why? Because we are subject to the vagaries of our audience's broadband connection, quality of their speakers etc. and all too often it can go wrong. The best, and most influential, audio visual should always be us, not the technology. I have learnt this from bitter personal experience when trying to play embedded animations and videos. The audience could not hear it, I could, but I wasn't able to view the audience so didn't realise what was going on. Honestly it was a mess. We must be fluent and rehearsed and very, very competent, otherwise it just comes across extremely poorly.

Most Slides Aren't Slides

Because they have too many words on them. Nancy Duarte[43], in her brilliant book *'Slideology'* [43] suggests that any slide with more than seventy-five words isn't a slide; it's a report. I think for what it's worth she has got a point. Slides need no more than thirty words so that they can be read and understood in less than three seconds. This is the concept of 'glance media', or as I always say, "our slides should look like a billboard which we drive past at eighty miles per hour on a foggy night". Slides must be visually easy on the eye and quick to comprehend.

Leverage The Ingredients Of An Effective Slide

Background: This is not the main event, it's the backdrop for the content which is displayed on it. Beware overly ornate or logo dense image for a backdrop. Do we want the audience working on the background or the information on it? The latter I would suggest.

Colour: We speak in a language of colour (e.g. "feeling blue, seeing red, green with envy, whiter than white etc.) therefore it matters as a choice. High contrast, where dark colour is combined with a light colour), is essential to make it easy to read, and this should be considered the absolute minimum. Low contrast makes our eyes work harder.

Images: Should be high quality, not stretched, thoughtful and relevant. We avoid bombarding a slide with a variety of different images because the viewer simply doesn't know where to look. My personal preference is for one really fabulous image, rather than multiple small images. Also, we do not need an image for every point and, if we are going to use more than one image, keep it in the same type of aesthetic. In other words, don't mix a photo with a drawing for example. Consistency is visually more soothing for the viewer. Finally, let's be more creative than the array of stock photos out there of impossible good-looking people doing ridiculous poses.

Text: Less of it and bigger so that it's visible and spaced out so that it's easier to read. There is much to say about the personality of fonts and some well-known global brands will tell us that different fonts have their own personality. A large font number and consistency throughout the slides is the key first goal to achieve here.

Arrange The Elements Of Our Slide Clearly

How we organise different elements of the slide (e.g. text, pictures, graphs etc.) is critical to determining whether or not the audience understand what they are looking at. So, the sorts of considerations we must address on our slides in a remote environment include:

Contrast: High contrast allows us to identify the point quickly. High contrast could be large and small font, italicised and non-italicised font, bold and not bold etc. Our eye is drawn to contrast, and we should always remember that as visual storytellers.

Flow: How we order the information given the direction our eye covers information matters here. For example, does our native language mean that we read left to right? Or right to left? Do we move top to bottom or bottom to top? What is the direction of travel for our eyes as we behold the slide? If we don't consider this when creating our slides, then it is quite simply a recipe for visual chaos.

Hierarchy: We look for relationships between items on a slide. Which items are connected to each other and which are more dominant?

Proximity: How close different pieces of information are to each other also causes the eye to stop and linger. The way we look at a slide is to understand connections between separate items, so if different pieces of information are very close together then we will look for a relationship between them. The point is this; put things close together that we want to create a connection with; otherwise, space them out.

Whitespace: Our eyes need it! This is what is called 'visual breathing room' and this is commonly challenged when professionals don't know if their slides are supposed to be slides or reports. Often this is not clear and we're trying to do both simultaneously. I would always argue that this is extremely difficult to do and would invite any leader to revert to their stakeholders to work out what the goals, preferences and priorities are for the digital asset we have been asked to create. If necessary, we should create real distinction between the part of our slide deck that is to be presented, versus the part that is for background or follow up reading.

In summary, and I'm mindful this is a topic about which I could write for a lot longer, it's how we organise these different components which will determine whether or not our audience understands the message we want to communicate. If I were to offer a summary of a brilliant, essential best practice: make our slides less visually dense and make them larger and easier to read. Getting three things right first would be superb.

Using Data On Slides

I have recently had a fascinating conversation with a leader who said: "the data speaks for itself". It never does. It is the story behind the data that counts, and visually, that's entirely our job to make clear. If we use data on slides it must:

- Be easy to read
- Have clear legends
- Use few pieces of data well; rather than lots of different pieces of data
- Highlight what's important using an arrow, a highlighted section etc. to draw the eye
- Have a 'so what?' For example, a graph of declining sales could have multiple consequence statements including 'we'll hit the bottom soon', 'this can't continue', 'the only way is up etc.' It is our responsibility to make the takeaway message abundantly clear to the audience, otherwise they will draw their own conclusions which might not be the same as ours.

All too often what I see on professional pitch decks are dense, hard to read pieces of data that are not clear regarding the message to be conveyed and as a result, often easily confuse and frustrate. As always, remember that this is a remote environment, *which means our audience are very easily distracted,* so we run an enormous risk to interest, attention and engagement if we don't seriously improve our skills here. Plus, they have seen lots of dreadful slide decks before ours, let's not be another forgettable one to add to the pile.

Presenting Persuasive Slide Decks

We're adding another dimension of communication to the remote environment when we use slide decks so there are some *essential* best practices to how we talk around them.

Why This Matters So Much

Quite simply because human beings can't simultaneously read and listen well. The experience for our audience is one of conflict: do I read what's on the slide? Or do I listen to what is being said? Being bombarded with both a lot to read and a lot to listen to *never, ever works well* if our goal is to influence others.

Remote Presence

Always Start With 'The 3 Ps'

Our audience needs to hear the purpose, process and payoff for the session. I have written about this elsewhere in the book and you, dear reader, may or may not have covered that chapter. Either way, I make no apology for re-working it here. We have all spent far too much time watching, not watching and listening, not listening to dull, boring, lengthy, confusing, complicated pitches. *We must* explain in the first thirty seconds the following pieces of information:

- *Purpose* – the goal for this pitch (a decision, action or commitment)
- *Process* – how we will do this (e.g. 'I have 3 slides; let me share them and then we'll have plenty of time for questions and yes, the slides will be shared' etc.) The point is that this is not typically made clear, so we have already lost our audience. We must, must, must do this properly and right at the beginning of our presentation.
- *Payoff* – what's the benefit to the audience of this? Again, if we don't make it clear, our audience are left to work it out for ourselves and often – they won't.

Sound Confident

Slow down, pause, avoid 'rubbish' and 'weasel' words, if we use three letter acronyms (TLAs) we should explain them the first time etc. We must pause to create anticipation and reflection, use metaphor and analogy that works across an international audience and inject energy, passion, belief, certainty into our delivery to engage others. In other words, everything I've written about elsewhere in this book does – unsurprisingly – apply here.

Keep Builds Down

Because they are a minefield. We are subject to the vagaries of the broadband connection, the technology platform we use, and our verbal message and the timely synchronization of the visual message can be very challenging to keep aligned. In addition, given that we may be feeling a degree of pressure at the moment of presenting our message, then it makes the challenge even greater. Keep it simple for our sanity and the sanity of our audience.

Don't Just Say What's On The Slides

We are not television newsreaders. It is intensely frustrating for the audience to hear the presenter only speak to the points which they can already read. It betrays a number of different problems (a) a lack of preparation (b) a lack of confidence (c) a lack of influence. If our only value is to articulate what the audience could perfectly well read, then we should just send the deck to our audience and they can decide for themselves whether or not they read it. Our role is much more important and profound. We have to add value in our verbal contribution; otherwise our audience will disengage. Passion, energy, commitment, authenticity, humour, humility, certainty, authority are all attributes that we can only powerfully convey through our verbal contribution, and it's much easier to leverage these verbal tools than try to make the slide do all the work.

Verbal Signposts Are Really Useful

To manage the audience when we present them visually with something that will be contentious, surprising or controversial. A verbal signpost is where we articulate what we are going to do next. For example, "I'm going to explain where these figures come from" or "let me talk about this year first, and then we'll go back to what last year's figures tell us". Or, 'I will cover the breakdown of the client base later on during this presentation'. Or, 'I will talk about the left hand set of figures on the slide and what that means, and then I'll cover the right hand set of figures". In other words, we are retain control of the audience and their reaction to our message by advising how we will address it in advance.

Orchestrate The Attention Of The Audience

By this I simply mean tell the audience where to look on the slide and trust me, they will obey without question. It's called the embedded command. So, when we direct the attention of the viewer by saying things like 'if you look at the picture on the right-hand side of the slide' for example, then our audience will automatically look there. The point here is that this is an extremely effective way of controlling the narrative or understanding taken from our slides and we always adopt this approach for our more complicated slides as a matter of course.

And Don't Forget To Rehearse

No matter how confident we feel and no matter how skilled we are, never, ever underestimate the importance of rehearsal of key messages when using PowerPoint remotely. Always remember, far too many presentations done remotely *are instantly forgettable and fail to influence.* We don't want that to be true for ours.

Chapter Eleven – The Dreaded Email

When I first thought about writing this book, I was determined not to put a chapter together about email; my mind was fixed on remote presence only. However, given the title of the book, it quickly became apparent that I could not leave the dreaded email out of it when it comes to being an effective remote communicator. Many would have us believe that email is dead, and yet here we are.

What changed my mind? The harsh reality that increasingly in this world of remote communication, email is still a primary source of communication, so it would be remiss of me to ignore it. Yes, I realise that a number of technology platforms are designed to encourage real-time collaboration that will reduce email traffic, however much of what I have written below still relates in these new environments.

Back to email for a moment: how many of us have ever found ourselves in a debate or conversation that becomes emotional? How often have we wished that an email trail would stop? Or perhaps that we shouldn't be involved in the email distribution list at all? The short answer must be all of us.

Fundamentally our challenge has to be the extent to which this medium of communication has become the *primary* means of building influence and relationships at work, and given that we all use the technology, this chapter is designed to offer some best practice strategies to honour, and common pitfalls to avoid. To be clear dear reader, the context for my observations is the fact that as leaders and influencers, our goal is to have impact, build our brand and be persuasive.

Which Medium And Which Message?

Who hasn't got enough emails at work? As of February 2017, 269 billion emails are sent every day[21], against a worldwide user group of 3.7 billion[21]. These are statistics that, by the time you have read them, will definitely be a long way out of date. Here are some more facts to contend with. An 'average' (if there ever is such a thing) office worker will receive 121[21] mails per day and will send around 40 business emails on a daily basis[21]. And perhaps we would like some more facts? Research from the Radicati Group[5] estimated that the number of emails sent per day in 2015 was in the order of **205 billion.** If that number isn't enough to make our eyes water, they further suggest that some **74 trillion** emails are sent every year, and this means **2.4 million emails per second**. And – the numbers will continue to rise, with email remaining the predominant form of communication in business. Wow. That's a lot of emails.

Certainly, my clients relate to a higher number than those quoted, and the trend upwards appears, for now, inevitable. We all live in an attention deficient economy, which means that if we're going to convey impact and screen presence through the most predominant medium of business communication, then this is something that requires our focus. So, let's do it now. Effectively our communication is made up of 3 parts:

(1) The Visual - how we look and our body language
(2) The Verbal - tone of voice, cadence, rhythm etc.
(3) The Words

We do not need Freud to appreciate that the most effective and complete form of communication is face-to-face because we can absorb or receive all of the communication. In addition, of course email gives us nothing *but the words.* We do not perceive the tonality, the visual, the energy, nothing. So, it is not surprising that the whole advent of emoticon symbolism was precisely to try to allay the potential for miscommunication. And of course, here's the point: if you have to think about or use an emoticon, then email is the wrong medium to communicate the message.

And not only has the medium of the message changed, but so has the world of the person receiving it. Remember that we live in an attention deficient economy. We sit in rooms, either together or apart, jump on calls and then profoundly and completely *not* listen to each other. We inhabit a world where two screens at least are the norm and as a result, our ability to get and retain the attention of others has never been more sorely tested. We are dreadful at it and we live in a world where that behavior is increasingly accepted.

So, what does that all of this mean? Quite simply, it is getting even harder to stand out, inspire others and communicate effectively. Compounding this challenge is the drive towards using a technology that can easily and readily *diminish* our impact if we don't develop the skills necessary to convey impact, develop trust and be persuasive by using it. We have to get to grips with this technology and hone our screen presence and if we don't, then we are in serious trouble.

A Common Cause

Amongst colleagues and clients alike, there are consistently common themes expressed with this technology. These include the extent to which we can become overwhelmed by the volume, the amount of time we spend 'pinging a note' to people during the day, the number of times we are caught up in a seemingly endless 'back and forth' of conversation, the pointless 'cc'ing activity that goes on when really it's a 'CYA' (Cover Your Ass) motive at play, and the wide range of emotions that range from mild irritation to outright fury at the content and tone of emails we receive.

There is little doubt that the level of emotional investment which the vast majority of professionals have in email causes us to have vocal, and overwhelmingly negative views about it, and all of this is set against the level of anxiety we might feel when we are unable to access our inbox for an extended period of time. And by this, I mean twenty minutes. Studies[21] also indicate that 86% of professionals choose email is their preferred means of communication, and yet equally I have yet to meet a *single person* who has ever suggested that they would want to talk less and email more.

As a consequence of these astonishing statistics and anecdotes, any book that talks about remote presence in a professional context needs to reference one of the primary digital tools on our screens that we use every single day to convey our virtual impact, hence the need to write about the dreaded email. What I have outlined here are first principles, rather than an exhaustive and extensive review of email best practice. Why? Because my fundamental rule is simple: *we're all in a relationship business and relationships don't get built on email.*

The Most Important Thing We Must Remember About Email

Remember, relationships don't get built here. Equally, relationships can get quickly destroyed by email. The capacity for electronic communication to elicit powerful emotions on a scale covering indignation, upset, rage, hurt, fury, sarcasm, frustration amongst other emotions, is immense. I speak from personal experience as I think of one person who emails me regularly and frankly, I have experienced all of the above and some other emotions too. Email is not the main purpose of our role, and I have yet to read a job description that lists it as a critical activity. However, we seem to be spending more and more time as keyboard warriors, so these are some of the most important first principles to consider in order to convey more remote presence and impact through your e-mail communication. So, let's start with some of the *absolute fundamentals.* By so doing and to be clear, whilst these may be the basics, how recently have you experienced these principles *not* being adhered to?

Does It Even Need To Be An Email?

Perhaps the first biggest opportunity to increase our screen presence is knowing when not to use it. More often than we might think the answer to this question is 'no'. A quick 'FYI' (For Your Information), or question that needs to be asked, or perhaps a short answer that needs to be provided, can easily be sent by text or direct messaging. One of my clients is an oil and gas business where I have an executive that I am coaching to make the next step in their career. Part of the comprehensive feedback which I gathered on his leadership effectiveness and executive presence specifically highlighted his over reliance on email. Time and again his essential stakeholder group commented on the need to pick up the phone and spend more time talking and less time typing.

To be clear, this insight is offered within a business that has a strong email culture, operates a flat organizational structure and where leaders are expected to deliver results across a horizontal, remote, global team. The drive to be agile, efficient, get things done and move on can all easily justify sending a lot of emails. However, we know relationships do not get built on email. We need to be careful that our drive to complete tasks and be operationally efficient doesn't supersede the *necessity* of building high calibre relationships. Talking to people is the only way to do that. A powerful operational rhythm which requires a different media for remote presence, is to set aside time during each day or week to hold short calls and remote meetings. They take much less time and vastly reduce the level of frustration that can be caused by table tennis email.

Start With Your Signature

Our email signature should reflect our personal brand. I am amazed at the number of emails I receive that simply don't have any signature at all. As a consequence, it's impossible to understand the role the sender holds in the organisation or work out the best way to contact the individual. Who wants to be anonymous and hard to contact? Our signature should be present on all our emails and advise the audience to know who we are and how to contact us. Given the challenges around enterprise wide servers, I would avoid lots of embedded graphics, images, hyperlinks and all sorts of other assets that can actually send our emails straight to our recipient's junk box, assuming they get through the company firewall in the first place.

Keep It Short

I have a client in the professional services area whom I was asked to work with because, amongst other things, their emails were renowned for their shoulder sagging length and complexity. Screens and screens of text in font size ten to twelve does not generally elicit joy and excitement on the part of the recipient. All too often they will think 'I don't have time to deal with this now' and 'I might get to it later or I might ignore it until you chase me'.

Always Complete The Subject Line

How many emails do you receive in a day? 50? 100? Never less than 200? How many of them have attachments? (Spreadsheets, PowerPoint slides? Reports?) 20%? 40%? Or is it higher? The point is that we all have to manage the competing demands and expectations of our clients and customers and can help each other out here. If we want our message to be heard, acted up and, most often responded to, then we must make clear what we want in the subject line. One of my clients gave me some fantastic insight years ago about this exact point. They wanted to refer to something I explicitly provided and, given that Outlook was their primary electronic filing system, wasted loads of time trawling through my emails one by one.

Beware of stating the obvious (e.g. 'report', 'question', 'hello' etc.) These are not very helpful – or inspiring. We want to *inspire* the recipient *to respond usually.* Sometimes it is more than that and even if *we don't want* the audience to respond, we need to make sure our email stands out to help increase the likelihood of it being seen, read, understood and where necessary, acted upon. Otherwise, what's the point of sending it? So, a more useful example might be 'Southern Team Data Report Requiring A Decision By Friday'. Or, 'I think I can help you out'. If you are concise, precise and let us know how low long we have to reply, it demonstrates self-awareness, competence and will more likely get us the response that we seek.

Beware Overuse Of The 'High Priority' Flag

Occasionally things are high priority, but most of the time most things are not. For me, the sight of a high priority flag on an email can elicit a reaction which starts with mild panic (did I miss something? Have I got to drop everything and do this now?). It moves to mild irritation if the answer to both those questions is 'no'. Why? Because we are all very busy and email is not the main purpose of our job.

Overuse of the high priory flag can convey a sense of either being massively disorganised and last minute, or it says that we can't prioritise and organise our time and requests for help properly, or it can say 'OMG I am having a meltdown and don't know what to do about it, so what I will do now is pass all my panic on to you'.

Stop The CYA Activity With The CC Or BCC

To cc or not to cc? Indeed, that is the question. What fascinates me in my work with clients is the emotion that is associated with the protocols used in this area. When reflecting on this particular topic for the purposes of writing about it in this book, I was curious about my own behaviour. I have noticed that the first thing I check is who else is copied in on the email – especially if there is an issue. I worry about whether or not the individual needs to be copied in, because I do not want to create unnecessary work or worry for them, plus I do not want to damage my own brand. Let's be honest; the human condition is such that we do not want others to see if feedback is negative and want the whole world to know if the feedback is positive.

Don't Always Hit 'Reply All' On A Group Email

I also note that my own preference is not to copy others in my reply. A particular pet peeve is when a group email goes out to let's say an audience of eighty people. It might be something innocuous regarding travel arrangements for a summit, or it might be something lovely such as to share an achievement of a colleague. What *I really cannot abide,* is being copied in on the 'well done!' or 'congratulations' replies. Or, 'I'm travelling from London via Reading and can you book a taxi for me?' We do not care about each other's replies of 'thanks Bob' sent in 78 dull and repetitive ways to Bob on his 78-person group email about offering to stay late to let the cleaners in the office. The simple fact is this: we are not interested!! The reply is not for our benefit and we should address our response to the sender, without feeling the need to let everyone else know, and we'll stop clogging up their inboxes at the same time.

Think About How You Start Your Note

Underestimate the first words written on your email at your peril. I have been working with a client this week who is *adamant* that if he/she just writes the recipient's name, so no use of 'Dear' or 'Hi' followed by the name, then it conveys fury, anger, or at the very least, irritation. Our view is that if our style has typically been to use 'Dear' or 'Hi', but then we do not do this, we need to be very careful because it can easily be interpreted as our getting upset or aggressive. Remember, email doesn't convey meaning well at all and as a result, we can all easily leap to conclusions that are often incorrect.

The key point is to be consistent. And when we talk about consistency, there are a couple of elements to it. The first is that we are consistent in use, so as not to cause anxiety or elevate the tension. The second reason is to ensure that our strategy is consistent with our brand values. There is some debate regarding whether or not a salutation such as 'hey' or 'hiya' is professional. My view is that it all depends on the cultural norms, the context for the email, our goal in sending it and so forth. All these things impact what the right opening words are to use. One thing I can say is that humour doesn't translate well. So, for example: "Morning Losers", which was honestly an opening I was shown on an email is stupid and wrong. We are at work. We can never delete it once we have written it. So let's just not do it.

CAPITAL LETTERS ARE NOT A GOOD IDEA

I have a colleague who uses capital letters – MOST OF THE TIME. I am unclear as to his motive, perhaps it is emphasis, perhaps it is an attempt to ensure that if I ignore everything else, then at least I will read the part in capital letters. Who knows? The point is that it reads as if he is shouting. And this DOES NOT TRANSLATE WELL WITH ME. My advice is to avoid the use of capital letters at all costs. It comes across as if we are shouting.

Don't Shoot From The Hip

Easy to say; much harder to do. Never, ever send an angry email, or give a quick, flippant or sarcastic response. I am mindful of this as I write this chapter because I have a colleague with whom I am involved in an email trail that is driving me crazy. I find him arrogant, narcissistic and fake, however other colleagues of mine do not share my opinion. I also think he is not that bright and feels easily threatened by even the most innocent question. Rather than immediately respond, draft a reply, leave it, come back to it later and only then respond, especially important if you're emotionally het up by the email. Send at haste but repent at leisure. A fail safe is simply to ask them to stop and repeat this request if they persist. This works in several ways; not least of which is that when we've all calmed down, it is in black and white that we have repeatedly tried to stop unproductive and frankly unhelpful activity on all sides.

The Use of Emoticons

If ever there was a digital solution that was created to acknowledge the pitfalls of emails then it is the emoticon. There is a vast swathe of images that can be used to convey happy face, a sad face, a furious face, a 'I looked like I swallowed my dentures' face, and so on. My view of emoticons is that if we feel we need to attach an emoticon to our message, it is usually because we do not wish the message to be mis-interpreted. The solution is simple: don't communicate the message by email and instead, pick up the phone or, even more radical, speak to them face-to-face.

The Use Of Exclamation Points

Can be really aggressive!!!!! And also really annoying!!!! It looks and reads like someone who is slightly out of control!!!!!! So, please, be careful!!!!!!!!!!!!!!!!!!!!!!!!!!

'But It Was Only A Joke'

This area is an absolute minefield. If our audience doesn't know us well, or if there are multiple recipients, or if our missive is going to be read by individuals for whom English isn't there first language, or, the list goes on and we get my point. The reality with humour is that it represents significant potential for miscommunication and possible offence being taken, so a good general rule is to take very good care. If in doubt: don't. I am not saying that we do not want to have humour in our work, because we do, and life is hard enough. I am not saying that humour is unprofessional, of course it's not, humour is a great way to create a moment of connection with others. I am not saying that we should always be very formal, professional and strait-laced, because that is not what we are anyway. And besides, laughing at ourselves is a fantastic source of humour and one of the most lovable of human qualities. What I *am saying* is that humour doesn't travel well on email. Our version of funny might not match that of our audience and they just don't get it. Worst case scenario is that we crash into the world of offending or upsetting others, which is never funny. So, exercise a large dose of care and caution. If we have to think twice about it, then the chances are it's funny enough to go in the email. So, don't put it there.

Do Proofread Your Message

Don't be surprised if we're judged by the way we compose an email. For example, if our email is littered with misspelled words and grammatical errors, we may be perceived as sloppy, careless, or even uneducated. *Always* check spelling, grammar and message before hitting the send button.

Don't Bother With The Recall Function In Outlook

How many of us have sent an email then instantly regretted it? I suspect all of us have. There is a piece of functionality that allows us to recall a message. However, this is really only a signal that the message was one we did not want to send. What email technology cannot do is remove the offending email from our inbox without us having seen it. If only. Candidly, whenever I see a recall message in my email, it is one of the quickest ways to spike my curiosity and encourage me to open it and find out what all the fuss was about. I would not bother with the recall function; and instead make a call to explain and clarify. Alternatively, we can send an email entitled 'update and request on last email'. Getting people to think about the future and the latest version is a more positive way to move forward.

Do Reply To All Emails

We should give a timely and polite reply to each legitimate email we receive. Even if we do not have an answer at the moment, take a second to write a response letting the sender know we received their email. Always advise the sender if their email was sent to the wrong recipient.

Check The Protocol For Sharing Sensitive Or Confidential Information Readily

I appreciate that we may have to share sensitive information electronically. However, password protecting it, sending a link to a password protected remote file via the cloud, hard copy, and checking with the sender regarding the right protocol are all great practices to avoid an unintentional data breach.

Don't Assume The Recipient Knows What We Are Talking About

Create our message as a stand-alone note, even if it is in response to a chain of emails. This means no 'one-liners.' Include the subject and any references to previous emails, research or conversations. It can be frustrating and time consuming to look back at the chain to brush up on the context. Our recipient may have hundreds of emails coming in each day and probably will not remember the chain of events leading up to our email.

Structure Your Email Into A Story

This means organising it into three parts, delineating each part (e.g. by emboldening it and making it a sub heading and using bullets). This makes our emails very quick and easy to read. Always have a clear ask and keep the length of our email limited to one screen. Avoid, avoid, avoid lots of lines, paragraphs and pages of text.

By way of example, take a look at what I mean below:

Example A

Bob,

There are several different ways we could go on this. I have been talking with Steffi and she agrees that we don't want to spend too much money this late in the fiscal period. The engineering team also wants to ensure that we can make it until the end of the year without any additional discretionary spend. All of this relates to our ability to hit key metrics for OTIF. I have researched a number of different options and it would seem that we can defer taking any action at all and simply ask the teams to focus on driving greater efficiency or finally we could change the metrics agreed for the last quarter in order to achieve what we need to by the end of the year. I have attached a number of league tables for you to review at your leisure and you can see that there are lots of issues to resolve. However, the opportunity is also there to make an impact before the end of the year. So, I attached three detailed analyses for you to read through and reach your own conclusions. There have been a lot of different contributions to what the issue might be and our biggest stakeholder, the AMO organisation, has been extremely vocal.

Their view was that at the beginning of the year the leadership team agreed metrics with a tolerance of less than 0.5% tolerance when it comes to OTIF delivery of materials for the Asia Pac region. As the data clearly shows, this is not entirely the case when it comes to performance and certainly not true if we look more broadly – and indeed on a global – scale. So, we have had several very constructive meetings with the AMO organization both remotely and face-to-face in order to see how we can address these concerned. Personally, I would like to see further discussions take place before making final recommendations.

It's important to note that we need to avoid confusion and ensure that the workload is carefully handled. One of the other issues to consider is the impact of Brexit now that the British government has finally decided to leave the European Union.

Very best wishes

Bob Mark Two

Example B

Bob,

The Problem We Face

- Increasingly concerns raised by our AMO/Materials organisation in the field due to misleading metrics/goals being published due to the global team directly approaching our people or requesting detailed action plans.
- This drives more workload, confusion on the PL strategy and challenges in focusing our attention also on the service levels.
- It's also impacting budget.

The Root Cause

- AMO has been tasked with hard inventory reduction goals, that forces them to get involved in our tactical strategies.
- They have no goals on Service levels or Tools WOP, driving an unbalanced attention to only one of our metrics.

Suggested Solution

- The Global Materials organisation should support our business in driving consistent processes.
- Policies and procedures shared across PL's should not be tasked to achieve a tactical goal, since will force them to get involved in our day to day business and misalign our priorities.

Do you agree?

Very best wishes
Bob Mark Three

There are clear differences between 'Example A' and 'Example 'B'. Length, clarity, structure, context, easy to read layout and a clear ask are just the most obvious distinctions. Looking at both emails causes us to be more ready to easily read, understand and action 'Example B', and somewhat wary and weary of reading 'Example A'. It is too long, the message is very unclear and there is no specific recommendation to resolve or 'ask' of the reader. It is what I would call 'a lot of weapons grade waffle'.

The Single Biggest Impact We Can Have With Email As Leaders....

Is to stop sending so many. We need to change our use of email within our business because whilst it is efficient, it is certainly not always effective. All too often I hear clients complaining about the amount of email traffic in their organisation. I sincerely believe that email is a cause of great stress, distraction and frustration in business today. However, my question is simply this: 'what are we doing to start to change it?' A follow up question is simply this: 'how much worse does it have to get before we choose to exercise more choice and more control in this situation?'

Challenging questions? Perhaps. And yet it is all too easy to fall into the trap of thinking that 'the business' or 'the industry' or 'the company' needs to change the culture around email, rather than us. It is all too easy to assume a kind of deflected sense of responsibility where emails are concerned. It is all too easy to play the hypocritical martyr. However, our job as leaders is to change things that don't work, to positively move the culture of a business, to choose and make our mission the things that will be better if we lead the charge to make it so. Email is precisely one of those things.

So, if we want to make a positive impact and enhance our remote presence, this is an excellent place to start, and remember to make it our mission to talk about it regularly to others. By so doing, they will start to join in with our approach and before we know it, there is a movement for change gathering momentum. That is leadership and that is presence; all done....remotely.

Bibliography

1. www.startrek.com
2. http://www.kaaj.com/psych/smorder.html
3. https://www.google.co.uk/about/company/
4. https://www.ofcom.org.uk/research-and-data
5. http://www.radicati.com/ *Email Statistics Report, 2013 – 2017*
6. https://www.laurenceolivier.com/
7. https://www.glamour.com/story/do-you-find-taller-men-more-at
8. *IBSG Economic and Research Insight: Andy Noronha and Joel Barbier*
9. https://hbr.org/2017/03/how-to-raise-sensitive-issues-during-a-virtual-meeting
10. Daniel Levitin: *The Organized Mind: Thinking Straight In The Age Of Information Overload*
11. https://www.sarahbrummitt.com/executive-training-development/the-books.aspx
12. https://www.inc.com/sims-wyeth/10-reasons-why-eye-contact-can-change-peoples-perception-of-you.html
13. *Steven Covey: Seven Habits of Highly Effective People*
14. *Robert Cialdini: The Psychology of Persuasion*
15. https://clausmoller.com/en/
16. *Ruby Wax:* https://youtu.be/FW1Kn3mw1s8
17. www.dictionary.cambridge.org
18. https://gls.london.edu
19. http://www.imdb.com/title/tt0116695/
20. *http://journals.plos.org/plosone/article?id=10.1371/journal.pone.0090779*
21. https://www.pressreader.com/uk/daily-star/20180501/282248076179378
22. https://www.amazon.co.uk/Predictably-Irrational-Hidden-Forces-Decisions/dp/0007256531
23. https://www.glamour.com/story/melania-trump-jacket-first-lady-wardrobe-meaning
24. https://tinyurl.com/y76t66oz
25. https://www.youtube.com/watch?v=GQN4On0K7-w
26. https://www.independent.co.uk/life-style/fashion/gareth-southgate-waistcoat-trend-how-to-world-cup-2018-england-manager-a8434916.html
27. http://www.deborahtannen.com
28. https://www.gwern.net/docs/psychology/1952-asch.pdf
29. https://theproductivitypro.com

Bibliography

30. https://www.imdb.com/title/tt0066721/

31. https://www.starwars.com

32. https://www.007.com

33. *Dan Ariel: Predictably Irrational*

34. http://www.brainrules.net

35. https://www.sunshinecoastdaily.com.au/news/channel-9-presenter-mocked-for-wearing-penis-jacke/3618573/

36. https://www.theguardian.com/politics/2020/feb/13/tracy-brabin-off-the-shoulder-dress-raises-20000-girlguiding

37. *Carol Kinsey Gorman: The Silent Language Of Leaders*

38. https://hbr.org/2013/01/the-price-of-incivility

39. https://www.skype.com/en/

40. https://www.zoom.us

41. https://www.insights.com/products/insights-discovery/

42. https://brenebrown.com

43. Nancy Duarte: *Slideology – The Art And Science Of Great Presentations*

44. https://news.cornell.edu/stories/2016/11/even-after-having-read-book-one-still-judges-it-its-cover